The Curious Incident of the Dog in the Night-Time
GCSE Student Edition

SIMON STEPHENS
Adapted from the novel by
MARK HADDON

with commentary and notes by
JACQUELINE BOLTON

Series Editor: Jenny Stevens

METHUEN DRAMA INDIA
BLOOMSBURY
NEW DELHI • LONDON • OXFORD • NEW YORK • SYDNEY

First published in India 2018
This stage adaptation first published in 2012 by Methuen Drama Published in this edition in 2016
Reprinted 2016 (three times), 2017 (twice), 2018

Adapted from the novel The Curious Incident of the Dog in the Night-Time by Mark Haddon, first published in 2003 by Jonathan Cape © Mark Haddon
All quotes from the stage adaptation of The Curious Incident of the Dog in the Night-Time by Simon Stephens, adapted from the novel by Mark Haddon, are reprinted with the permission of Bloomsbury Publishing Plc

Methuen Drama India
An imprint of Bloomsbury Publishing Plc
BLOOMSBURY, Methuen Drama India and the Methuen Drama logo are trademarks of Bloomsbury publishing Plc

This edition published with permission from Bloomsbury Publishing Plc,
50 Bedford Square, London, WC1B3DP, UK

A catalogue record for this book is available from the British Library.
A catalog record for this book is available from the Library of Congress.

ISBN 978 93 88038 59 1
10 9 8 7 6 5 4 3 2 1
For sale in the Indian subcontinent only

Bloomsbury Publishing India Pvt. Ltd
Second Floor, Building No. 4
DDA Complex LSC, Pocket C – 6 & 7
Vasant Kunj, New Delhi 110070
www.bloomsbury.com

Series: GCSE Student Editions

Typeset by RefineCatch Limited, Bungay, Suffolk
Printed and bound in India by Thomson Press India Ltd.

Contents

Commentary

Playwright

Simon Stephens was born in Stockport, Greater Manchester, in 1971. Between 1989 and 1992 he studied History at the University of York. During this period he wrote and directed a handful of plays, two of which – *Good Rocking Tonight* and *Duke* – he took to the Edinburgh Fringe Festival. Upon graduating, he spent two years in Edinburgh before moving to London in 1994. He managed the theatre bar at Riverside Studios, Hammersmith, before deciding to train as a teacher. Stephens continued to write plays throughout this period and in December 1998 his ninth play, *Bluebird*, secured his first professional production at the Royal Court (Theatre Upstairs), London.

Stephens was working as a secondary school teacher in Dagenham, Essex, when he was appointed Playwright in Residence at the Royal Court in 2000. He was Playwright in Residence at the Royal Manchester Exchange in 2001 and at the National Theatre in 2005. From 2000 to 2005 he was the Writer's Tutor for the Royal Court's Young Writers' Programme and taught playwriting in local schools. He also held playwriting workshops with inmates of HMP Wandsworth and HMP Grendon and worked with Youth Offending Teams in London and Salford. He is currently Artistic Associate at the Lyric Hammersmith, London, and Associate Playwright at the Royal Court.

Since committing full-time to writing in 2000, Stephens has (as of September 2015) produced twenty-one original plays and six adaptations, making him one of the most prolific writers of his generation. Awards include the Pearson Award for Best New Play (*Port*, 2002); the Olivier Award for Best New Play (*On The Shore of the Wide World*, 2005); and the *Manchester Evening News* Award for Best Production (*Punk Rock*, 2009). His plays, which are produced across Europe and, increasingly, Canada and the United

States, have been translated into over a dozen languages. They are frequently performed in Germany and he has won the prestigious *Theater Heute* Award for Best Foreign Play on three occasions (*Motortown*, 2007; *Pornography*, 2008; and *Wastwater*, 2011).

In 2015, *Funfair*, Stephens's adaptation of Austro-Hungarian playwright Ödön von Horváth's 1932 play *Kasimir and Karoline*, was the opening production of Manchester's new arts centre, HOME Manchester. Other adaptations include *The Trial of Ubu* (2012) adapted from *Ubu Roi* by Alfred Jarry, *The Cherry Orchard* (2014) by Anton Chekhov and *A Doll's House* by Henrik Ibsen, which in 2013 transferred from the Young Vic to the Duke of York Theatre in London's West End. *The Curious Incident of the Dog in the Night-Time* is Stephens's first stage adaptation of a novel and the first of his plays to transfer to Broadway.

Themes

Difference

At the centre of *The Curious Incident of the Dog in the Night-Time* is a teenage boy whose abilities and behaviour – his difficulty with reading people's faces or body language, for example, and preference for being alone; his aptitude for maths and physics and aversion to the colours yellow and brown – correspond to traits associated with autism (see 'Context'). While his condition is never explicitly diagnosed, the opening episodes of the play swiftly establish that Christopher John Francis Boone, who is 'fifteen years and three months and two days' (33) and knows 'every prime number up to 7507' (32), is *different*: he curls up and groans when frightened or under pressure; he screams and lashes out when touched; and he will not take off his watch because of an obsessive need to 'know exactly what time it is' (35).

Christopher is labelled as 'different' because he behaves in ways that are regarded as 'socially unacceptable'. Some of his actions are unacceptable because they threaten to harm another individual, such as when he gets into fights at school or throws things in anger. Mostly, however, Christopher's behaviour seems odd because it does not conform to commonplace assumptions of how a 'normal' fifteen-year-old boy should act. *Curious Incident* not only considers what it is to be 'different' but also depicts how others react when confronted with 'difference'. Christopher looks like a teenage boy – almost a young adult – so when his behaviour imitates that of a child, the adults in the play typically mock him or become angry. Nicola Walker, who played Christopher's mother in the 2012 National Theatre production, thinks that *Curious Incident* is about:

> how you are treated when you do not behave in socially acceptable ways – and also about how we are all, all of us, somewhere on that scale. We all have to negotiate social norms; some of us are better at negotiating social norms than others and that is okay.[1]

Curious Incident asks us to reflect upon our own attitudes towards 'difference' and to question 'common-sense' ways of seeing the world.

Facts

Christopher makes sense of the world strictly through facts, logic and reason, which to him are far more tangible than emotions and feelings. For him, the ordered sequences and repeatable equations of science and maths offer a safe space of certainty and stability distinct from the messy complications of human relationships and social interaction. He derives solace from thinking about physics, astronomy and the universe and, at times of anxiety, withdraws into his own world of numbers – doubling twos or counting the cubes of cardinal numbers – in order to comfort, reassure and calm himself down. His love of solving puzzles via deductive logic means that his mind is fired by the mystery of 'Who Killed Wellington?', and it is this mystery which sets in motion the events of the play.

For Christopher, 'truth' is equivalent to a reality that can be observed, measured and tested by our senses (what we call 'empirical reality'). His perception and understanding of the world is very literal and he has difficulty understanding figurative language (language which refers to something other than its 'proper

1 Nicola Walker, interview with Jacqueline Bolton, London, 27 July 2015.

meaning', such as metaphor, slang or sarcasm). He does not tell lies, he tells us, not because he is 'a good person' but because he *can't*: Christopher's computer-like mind is *unable* to pretend that something happened when, in reality, it didn't. Christopher's inability to tell lies – and his instinctive aversion to them – contrasts sharply with the centrality of secrets and lies to the plot of *Curious Incident*.

Fiction

> **Christopher** The word metaphor means carrying something from one place to another and it is when you describe something by using a word for something that it isn't [. . .] I think it should be called a **lie**. (39)

As discussed above, figurative language such as metaphor confuses Christopher because he attempts to make literal sense of the phrase ('imagining an apple in someone's eye doesn't have anything to do with liking someone a lot' [39]). For Christopher, because a metaphor is not factually 'real' this means that it is not 'true' and should, therefore, be regarded as a lie. Christopher reserves the same harsh judgement for the theatre – something we might consider as a live, four-dimensional metaphor – towards which he is intensely suspicious: 'I don't like acting because it is pretending that something is real when it is not really real at all so it is like a kind of lie' (82). Christopher does not understand that fictional creations of the imagination – like drama, fiction, and poetry – can also be useful tools (alongside science, maths and logic) with which to make sense of the world. As Siobhan tries to explain to him: 'people like stories, Christopher. Some people find things which are kind of true in things which are made up' (82).

Curious Incident is a work of fiction which itself reflects on the power of stories, of 'things which are made up', to reveal truths about human experience. Interestingly, we might observe that the importance of play – of imaginatively engaging in a fictional world – is indeed central to its plot, as represented by the train set which is bought for Christopher. As Judy recounts in one of her letters, Christopher played with this train set 'for weeks and weeks and weeks' on end:

> **Judy** We told you about train timetables [. . .] and you had a clock and you made the train run on time. And [. . .] we showed you how people who wanted to go on a train went to the station and bought a ticket and then got on a train. (73)

Particularly (but not exclusively) for young children, 'playing' – freely exploring the imagination, without adult direction or guidance – is central to our understanding of, and negotiation with, the world and our place within it. In this instance, Christopher's imaginative engagement with his train set has quite literally prepared him for a journey to London which is otherwise a terrifying ordeal for him. Because Christopher has already 'rehearsed' this journey by playing with his toy train set, he is better equipped to embark upon this journey 'in real life'. In this, and other ways, *Curious Incident* celebrates the role of the imagination in understanding the realities of the world in which we live.

Fallibility of adults

To be fallible is to be capable of making mistakes. It is a trait shared by everyone – indeed, it is what makes us human. Growing up, however, it can often come as a surprise to learn that adults, our parents or guardians in particular, are *not in*fallible: that despite their advanced years(!), they too can make mistakes, behave badly and fail in their relationships.

The background to the events of *Curious Incident* is Ed and Judy Boone's two-year separation. Judy left the family home because she found it difficult to cope with Christopher's behaviour and believed that he and Ed would be better off without her. At a loss to know what to do, and in an attempt to protect Christopher from the truth, Ed told him his mother had died. With Christopher's discovery of Wellington, Ed has a second secret to try and keep from his son. Ed fears that Christopher might discover the truth about not only Wellington but also his mother and so does all he can to prevent this from happening. While well-intentioned, Ed becomes trapped by his own lies and his attempt to protect Christopher backfires spectacularly. Interestingly, Christopher's compulsive honesty throws into relief the uneasy relationship to truth displayed by the adults around him, exposing the vulnerabilities and frailties of adult relationships.

Things to remember

You can read a more extensive and developed discussion of all these themes in the accompanying Study Guide to the play.

Characters

Christopher

Christopher is a fifteen-year-old boy with behavioural difficulties who lives with his father, Ed, in Swindon.

As discussed in 'Themes' and 'Context', Christopher's behaviour and abilities correspond to traits commonly associated with autism. Christopher often displays an emotional disconnect from his immediate surroundings but – as when he explains the Milky Way to his dad (36), or leaps into a fantasy about becoming an astronaut (53) – it is clear that his mind is alert, inquisitive and incredibly agile. His intelligence is demonstrated in several elegant speeches, as when he considers the universe as composed of 'billions of stars' rushing away from one another after the Big Bang:

> **Christopher** And when the universe has finished exploding all the stars will slow down, like a ball that has been thrown into the air and they will come to a halt and they will all begin to fall towards the centre of the universe again [. . .] faster and faster and we will know that the world is going to end soon because [. . .] there will be no darkness, just the blazing light of billions and billions of stars, all falling. (37)

Christopher likes reason and logic and solving puzzles and this is how he makes sense of the world. Indeed, presented with the mystery of 'Who Killed Wellington?', Christopher, for all his young naiveté, is as unswervingly logical and coolly unsentimental as his fictional hero, Sherlock Holmes:

> **Christopher** Why would you kill a dog? [. . .] I think you would only kill a dog if you (a) you hated the dog or (b) if you were mad or (c) because you wanted to make Mrs Shears upset. I don't know anybody who hated Wellington so it if was (a) it was probably a stranger. I don't know any mad people either, so it if was (b) it was also probably a stranger [. . .] But most murders are committed by someone known to the victim. In fact, you are most likely to be murdered by a member of your own family on Christmas Day.
>
> **Siobhan** Is that a fact?
>
> **Christopher** Yes actually it is a fact. Wellington was therefore most likely to have been killed by someone known to him. I only know one person who didn't like Mrs Shears and that is Mr Shears [. . .] This means that Mr Shears is my Prime Suspect. (50)

Statistics, facts and logic are reassuring to Christopher, in contrast to social interaction which he finds very difficult. People are 'confusing' to Christopher; firstly, because he finds it difficult to interpret facial expressions and, secondly, because people 'often talk using metaphors' – that is, using words or phrases that mean one thing to mean or suggest something else (39). Christopher's computer-like mind struggles to comprehend 'information' that requires *interpretation*, or the use of *social imagination*, in order to understand what someone means – as when someone raises an eyebrow to indicate they are unimpressed, or uses figurative language for colour and emphasis: 'it was a real pig of a day'. Christopher finds it hard to interpret meanings that are *implied* rather than explicitly stated and banter is completely lost on him, as when he sharply corrects Rhodri's jokey description of his 'little bottle of red paint':

> **Christopher** It's not red paint, it's red food colouring because I don't eat yellow food. If you put red paint into a curry it would be extremely dangerous and it would probably kill you. (61)

Christopher finds it difficult to empathize with the emotions that cause other people to behave in certain ways. As Niamh Cusack, who played Christopher's teacher, Siobhan, in the 2012 National Theatre production, puts it:

> what Christopher can't get his head around is the complexity of human relationships – and particularly the pressure his existence puts on his parent's marriage. That's not something he can engage with – he can engage in a much more tangible way with the universe.[2]

We also, however, see Christopher struggle to interpret and process his own emotional responses, as when he discovers his mother's letters, for example, or learns that it was his father who killed Wellington. While Christopher's emotions are turbulent, as the play progresses he develops an increasing confidence and maturity. The clearest example of this is the courage he demonstrates in venturing beyond his familiar surroundings to find his mum in London. Making this journey forces him to talk to strangers, confront the chaos of train stations, negotiate the tube and navigate the streets of London; for Christopher these situations represent significant personal challenges which he must overcome if he is to reach his mother's flat. That he successfully finds his way to Willesden is a testament to Christopher's determination and strength, qualities that perhaps he didn't know he even possessed.

Ed

Ed Boone, a plumber who lives in Swindon, is Christopher's father. He is separated from Christopher's mother, Judy.

The story of *Curious Incident* begins two years after Ed and Judy's separation. This has been a tough time for Ed: his wife has left him for another man, his subsequent relationship with Mrs Shears has ended badly and he is single-handedly raising a child with social and behavioural problems. Indeed, the first time we see Ed, he is picking up Christopher from the police station; his repeated

2 Niamh Cusack, interview with Jacqueline Bolton, London, 27 July 2015.

requests for Christopher to 'stay out of trouble' suggest not only the frequency with which Christopher gets into trouble but also the strain that this places on Ed. An important clue to understanding his character is provided by Judy in one of the letters she writes to Christopher: 'I'm not like your father', she writes, 'Your father is a much more patient person. He just gets on with things and if things upset him he doesn't let it show' (74). Just as Christopher struggles to interpret and process his feelings, Ed finds it difficult to express his emotions, preferring instead that they be ignored or buried. When Ed attacks Wellington with a garden fork, this is a direct consequence of the anger and frustration that he has been suppressing for some time: 'Maybe if I'd just given it a kick it would probably have backed off', he admits in retrospect. 'But, shit Christopher, when the red mist comes down . . . [it] was like everything I'd been bottling up for two years just . . .' (79).

Ed begins the play by thinking that the best way to cope with difficult situations is to cover them up and bury his emotions. His fears that Christopher might discover the truth about his mother (combined with his frustration at Christopher's un-cooperative behaviour) find expression in a series of increasingly angry exchanges which end in a physical fight between father and son. This fight demonstrates the lengths to which Ed will go in order to protect his son from discovering that his mother left him, but it also reveals the extent to which Ed has become trapped by his own lies. By the end of Part One Ed realizes that his strategy has created more problems than it has solved and that, in order to rescue their relationship, he must tell Christopher the whole truth. This moment is a turning-point for Ed as, for the first time, he faces the consequences of the ill-judged decisions he made in moments of crisis.

Ed presents a complex character study. While he has many flaws, these should be weighed against both the challenges of caring for a child whose needs are as difficult as Christopher's and the love which – although at times clumsily expressed – Ed clearly feels for his teenage son. His devotion to Christopher is consistent and can be observed in seemingly mundane daily activities: he prepares Christopher's often eccentric choice of meals; he looks out for programmes that Christopher will like and asks after his day at school. Ed is neither as articulate nor as academically gifted as his son but he recognizes and appreciates Christopher's prodigious mathematical gifts and insists, despite Mrs Gascoyne's protests, that Christopher take his Maths A-Level. Few of Ed's efforts are acknowledged or reciprocated by Christopher, who shares no interests with his father, prefers to be alone and will not be touched, let alone hugged. Ed's love, however, is unconditional and, throughout the course of Part Two, he demonstrates an unwavering commitment to regaining the trust of his son.

Judy

Judy Boone is Christopher's mother. She left Ed and Christopher to live with Roger Shears in London two years ago.

Judy is introduced to us through Christopher's memories and her letters. We first glimpse her when Christopher remembers a family holiday in Cornwall. She is on the beach at Polperro, where she is sunbathing, swimming, encouraging Christopher to paddle in the sea and playfully fantasizing about a Mediterranean lover. Christopher's memory suggests that Judy is someone who is full of energy, highly sensual (she will drink red wine, bask in the sun and smoke French cigarettes with her lover) and, perhaps, a bit of a dreamer.

In her letters to Christopher, Judy describes herself as 'not a very good mother' (74). She provides a candid account of how difficult it was to deal with his behaviour and describes how her continued frustration and feelings of self-doubt led to arguments with Ed. Feeling lonely in her marriage, Judy began an affair with Mr Shears (their neighbour) but was not willing to leave Christopher. After an incident where her toes were broken by Christopher throwing a chopping board, however, Ed took over Christopher's care. 'I remember looking at the two of you' she writes, 'and thinking how you were really different with him. Much calmer. And it made me so sad because it was like you didn't need me at all' (76).

Having persuaded herself that to leave would be 'the best for all of us' (76), Judy, like Ed, is trapped by her own decision. Although Christopher doesn't know this when the play opens, over the past two years Judy has written him forty-three letters: that she misses her son very much is evident from not only the number of letters but also the details she includes (see 73–77). Judy is overjoyed when Christopher turns up on her doorstep and, once reunited, is determined to keep Christopher with her: she has a stand-up argument with Ed and dictates to a peeved Roger that Christopher will be staying with them indefinitely. Theirs is not a fairy-tale reunion, however: despite her best efforts, Judy continues to find dealing with Christopher's challenging behaviour extremely difficult. Christopher's habit of going for walks by himself at night throws her into an extreme panic and she admonishes him roughly: 'If you ever to that again, I swear to God, Christopher, I love you but . . . I don't know what I'll do' (116). Under pressure from both Ed and Roger, the added strain of Christopher's repeated pleas to sit his Maths A-Level pushes Judy to breaking point: 'Christopher I am just about holding this together. But I am this close to losing it, all right?' (117). Judy postpones Christopher's A-Level to give herself some breathing space but this only results in him throwing a tantrum on Hampstead Heath. Judy is eventually defeated by Christopher's obstinacy and rearranges for him to sit the exam.

Judy, like Ed, has her flaws. She can, in her own way, be as stubborn as Christopher and, at the close of the play, is still learning how to reconcile the conflict between her own and Christopher's needs. When given a second chance to be a mother to Christopher, however, Judy seizes the opportunity and determines to persevere.

Siobhan

Siobhan is Christopher's teacher. It is at her suggestion that Christopher writes the book that becomes the play (see 'Dramatic devices').

The play reveals very little biographical detail about Siobhan: we do not know where she lives, whether she is married or whether she has children. She exists only in relation to Christopher, for whom she provides a kind of sanctuary: a safe space removed from the messy emotions and tangled lies of his parents. With Siobhan, Christopher plays, learns, thinks, imagines and makes hypotheses as to the identity of Wellington's killer. The most sustained conversations Christopher has are with Siobhan: he confides in her, remembers his mother with her, and sometimes chats to her in his head, as when he goes for a walk in London at night (114–117). In turn, Siobhan offers

Christopher support, encouragement, reassurance and inspiration. She is the only character with a window into Christopher's mind, and the only character who can speak to Christopher about his maths: 'What's the logarithmic formula for the approximate number of prime numbers not greater than x?' she asks, as she attempts to get his brain working before his A-Level (124).

Up until Christopher is reunited with Judy, Siobhan is the central female figure in his life. They share a bond of affection and trust that is unique to them; indeed, at certain moments in the play, Siobhan narrates Christopher's book as though *she* were Christopher speaking – 'she becomes the soul of Christopher', as actress Niamh Cusack suggests. Siobhan always tells Christopher the truth, even if this truth is sometimes unwanted, uncomfortable or troubling to him. Indeed, Siobhan's refusal to mislead or lie to Christopher generates the crackling tension in the play's final moments, as she remains silent in the face of Christopher's repeated questioning:

> **Christopher** Does that mean I can do anything, do you think?
>
> Does that mean I can do anything, Siobhan?
>
> Does that mean I can do anything? (130)

Siobhan is clear-sighted and realistic about Christopher's long-term prospects, and she would rather be honest than offer him the cheap comfort of false hope. As Cusack points out, Siobhan is 'the person who never lies to Christopher. That last moment in the play is so poignant because of that, because she's so honest with him. I think that is what's so great about her, she doesn't give easy answers.'

Things to do

From the list below, choose five words that you think best describe each character. Find a line from the text to support or evidence each of your choices.

Affectionate Ambitious Anxious Aggressive Afraid
Bitter Bold Calm Caring Childish Cold Competitive
Creative Deceitful Despairing Difficult Dishonest
Energetic Free Generous Guilty Guarded Intelligent
Inquisitive Irresponsible Irritable Jealous Kind Lonely

Loving Maternal Misguided Obstinate Open-minded
Patient Playful Prejudiced Protective Proud Relaxed
Resentful Resilient Responsible Restless Restricted
Sensible Strong Stubborn Troubled Worried
Warm Weak Wise

Context

Around the play

The Curious Incident of the Dog in the Night-Time (2003) is a novel by Mark Haddon. It is written from the first-person perspective of a fifteen-year-old boy, Christopher John Francis Boone, who is writing the book for a school project. Prompted by the discovery of a dead dog in his neighbour's garden, Christopher's attempts to find the murderer develops into a more complex journey of self-discovery. Although never explicitly stated, from Christopher's narration we understand that his behaviour – his difficulties with understanding emotions and reading people's faces; his dislike of being touched; his obsessive detailing and explanations; his aptitude for maths and physics – is that of a teenager who is autistic. While the book that Christopher is writing focuses on solving the mystery of 'Who Killed Wellington?', it becomes clear that the real subject of the novel by Mark Haddon is Christopher himself. *The Curious Incident of the Dog in the Night-Time* was an instant success with both adults and younger readers, selling over two million copies and winning the Whitbread Book of the Year and the *Guardian* Children's Fiction Prize.

Simon Stephens's stage adaptation of *The Curious Incident of the Dog in the Night-Time* premiered at the National Theatre, London, on 2 August 2012, directed by Marianne Elliot. It was enthusiastically received by audiences and critics, and transferred to the Apollo Theatre in London's West End in March 2013. In that year it won an incredible seven Olivier Awards (which recognize excellence in professional productions staged in London) including Best New Play, Best Director and Best Actor for Luke Treadaway's performance as Christopher. In October 2014, the National Theatre production made its debut on Broadway, New York, at the Ethel Barrymore Theatre.

The production opened to rave reviews and won a clutch of awards, including six Tony Awards (the US equivalent of Olivier Awards).

Within the play

In the words of Mark Haddon, the greatest challenge presented by turning the novel into a play was how to 'tell the story from outside Christopher's head without losing something really important about his peculiar view of the world from inside it' (quoted in Bunyan and Moore, 2013: 127). The dramatic form does not enable us to get inside Christopher's head in the way that the novel permits; instead, we have to listen to what he says and watch what he does in order to work out what he is thinking and feeling. The same is true of the people around Christopher. We do not experience the characters of Siobhan, Ed, Judy and others through the filter of Christopher's mind but instead have to interpret the behaviour and actions of those characters ourselves.

Aside from the necessary shift from the subjective 'first-person' viewpoint of the novel to the objective 'third-person' viewpoint of the stage, Stephens's adaptation is extremely faithful to the narrative, characters and environments described in Haddon's novel. While the action is condensed for effective story-telling, Christopher remains the central protagonist. Just like the novel, the play is created from the book that he writes: it is *his* story and *his* world that is created onstage.

Although Christopher's condition is never named in either the novel or the play, he does display behavioural traits associated with autism and, in the early publications of the novel, is described on its cover as having Asperger's Syndrome. Autism can be understood as a type of developmental disability, meaning that individuals may have problems developing intellectual, physical, learning, language and/or behavioural skills. Autism is a 'spectrum condition' which means that it can differ widely from person to person: no two people with autism will face the same challenges.

According to Ambitious about Autism, a UK-based charity that campaigns to change policy and practice for children and young people with autism, the difficulties autism can create may be grouped into two main categories: **social communication/interaction** and **repetitive behaviours and activities**.

Social communication/interaction

People with autism can find it very difficult to talk to and socialize with other people, often preferring to be by themselves. Understanding jokes, metaphors, sarcasm and other subtleties, such as hints or irony, can be difficult because they understand language literally (directly according to its proper meaning), not figuratively (referring to something other than its 'proper meaning'). People with autism may take instructions very literally; indeed, Christopher complains to Siobhan that 'people often say "Be quiet" but they don't tell you how long to be quiet for' (43). They may have an excellent vocabulary but, as inflection and expression are socially learned, they can find it hard to manage the tone of their voice and so sound robotic or monotonous.

It is often very hard for people with autism to read nonverbal cues, such as facial expressions and body language (Christopher finds people 'confusing' because they 'do a lot of talking without using any words' [34]). As a result, they can seem oblivious or callous – although in reality they have simply missed or misread the signals. People with autism are often described as 'lacking empathy' but this can be misunderstood. It is not necessarily that they *can't* 'feel' for, or empathize with, others but that autism interferes with the ability to both notice and interpret other people's feelings. This is a skill technically described as 'social imagination'. Even if a person with autism can tell what someone else is feeling, s/he may not know how to respond to them appropriately. Some people with Asperger's, however, may be entirely comfortable with themselves: their interests satisfy them and their difficulties don't interfere with anything they want to do, meaning that problems with social interaction may not feel like a serious loss.

Repetitive behaviours and activities

People with autism may be prone to developing rules and rituals; Christopher, for instance, believes that seeing four red cars in a row on the way to school makes it a 'Good Day' and that a Good Day is a day for 'projects and planning things' (42). Other rules might involve disliking particular colours, or refusing – no matter how hungry – certain kinds of food because of their texture or colour (Christopher will not eat food that is yellow). People with autism can get very attached to doing things the same way each time, and can get extremely upset if their routines are disturbed.

As well as being inclined to rules and rituals, it is common for a person with autism to have difficulty processing the information that their eyes, ears, nose, muscles and skin are sending to the brain. These sensory difficulties are basically a question of certain senses being either hypersensitive (oversensitive) or hyposensitive (under sensitive). If a sense is 'amplified' ('turned up') in a person with autism, they will be vulnerable to 'overstimulation' and may become physically and mentally overwhelmed (see Christopher's experiences at Swindon and Paddington Stations).

According to the Office of National Statistics, one in one hundred children is diagnosed with autism. Its cause is not known but is most likely to stem from the interaction of various factors: genetic, neurological and psychological. While many learn to manage the more stressful aspects of their condition and acclimatize to social rules, even the most independent people are still dealing with a complicated condition. Early intervention and the right help can be incredibly important. For more information on autism, including advice, support and links to related organizations, visit www.ambitiousaboutautism.org.uk.

While it is useful and necessary to be informed about autism when engaging with *Curious Incident*, it is worth remembering Mark Haddon's assertion that it is 'not a book about Asperger's [. . .] it's a novel about difference, about being an outsider, about seeing the world in a surprising or revealing way' (see 'Themes').[3] It is important to remember that neither the novel nor the play provide a medically authoritative reference guide to autism. Christopher is a *fictional character* imagined by his authors so that we, as readers and as spectators, might 'imagine other possibilities and explore other [. . .] worlds' which might otherwise remain unfamiliar and inaccessible to us.[4]

3 Mark Haddon, 'asperger's and autism', *Mark Haddon*, 16 July 2009: http://www.markhaddon.com/aspergers-and-autism [accessed 18 August 2015].

4 Simon Stephens, *Plays: Three* (London: Methuen, 2011), p. viii.

Dramatic devices

Structure

Curious Incident is structured into Part One and Part Two, each of which contains many different episodes, or 'chunks of action', which follow one after the other. These episodes – some of which are very short, some of which cover several pages – are not formally divided into individual scenes (e.g. 'Act 1, Scene 2', or 'Act 2, Scene Five'): the action does not stop and start with the ending and beginning of each episode but is instead continuous. Once the play has begun, the action does not stop until the end of Part One, where the interval falls; similarly, once Act Two is underway the stage is in constant motion until the lights fall on Siobhan and Christopher. At this point, however, the play is not quite finished. After the curtain call, Christopher returns with a treat for the audience: the 'Postscript', or 'Maths Appendix', where he demonstrates how he solved his favourite A-Level Maths question.

An important point to note about the play's structure is that the events of Part One are not presented in chronological order. The arrangement of time is not linear; instead, the story jumps backwards and forwards between Christopher's discovery of Wellington and his decision to write a book about it. Episodes can take place in different times and locations simultaneously (the opening scene is a good example of this), there are flashback scenes between Ed and Christopher, and a 'memory' scene in which Christopher remembers his mother. There are, moreover, moments when the narrative seems momentarily suspended, as when Christopher imagines being an astronaut or explains why he finds people confusing. These moments might seem like unnecessary or confusing digressions from the main narrative but in fact they provide us with insights into Christopher's mind, and reveal to us something of how he perceives the world. Part Two is slightly more straightforward: after the opening scene introduces the framing device of 'a play within a play' (see below), Christopher's personal odyssey to London and all further narrative events are presented in the chronological order in which they occur.

Another aspect of the play to note is that it contains a mixture of narrated and enacted action. As Part Two reveals, the play we are watching onstage is adapted from the book that (at Siobhan's suggestion) Christopher writes about his investigation into 'Who Killed Wellington?' In Part One, the character of Siobhan narrates this story while the ensemble – the rest of the acting company apart from the actors playing Christopher, Ed and Judy – act out the characters that Christopher writes about in his book. In the original National Theatre production, ten actors played forty-one speaking parts between them! The use of an ensemble of actors to multi-role a variety of characters encourages an appreciation of the skill and technique involved in putting on a play, producing a heightened sense of theatricality particularly apt for a play which is partly about the act of putting on a play. Part Two opens with the following conversation between Siobhan and Christopher:

> **Siobhan** Christopher, I want to ask you something. Mrs Gascoyne has asked if we would like to do a play this year. She asked me to ask everybody if we'd like to make some kind of performance for the school [. . .] I was wondering if you'd like to make a play out of your book. Everyone could join in and play a part in it. [. . .]
>
> **Christopher** No. It's a book and it's for me and not everybody, just for me.
>
> **Siobhan** I know that Christopher, but I think a lot of people would be interested in what would happen if people took your book and started acting bits out of it. (82)

Stephens is here treating the audience in the theatre to a playful meta-theatrical joke, as 'people [. . .] acting bits out' of Christopher's book is precisely what we, the audience, have been watching throughout Part One! Christopher's negative response – 'No. I don't like acting because it is pretending that something is real when it is not really real at all so it is like a kind of lie' (82) – is funny not only because we realize that, in the end, Christopher did not get his way (his book *has* been turned into a play for 'everyone' to 'join in' with) but also because 'Christopher' is himself being played by an actor who is acting a character who is deeply suspicious of acting! Christopher's dislike of acting reminds us of his singularly literal engagement with the world and the people around him. The play continues to highlight this trait as Christopher repeatedly draws attention to the fact that he, Christopher, is not only acting in but also *directing* the play made from his book. As actor Luke Treadaway, who played Christopher in the 2012 National Theatre production, puts it: 'Christopher doesn't like lying at all so [we figured that] the only way he'd be able to tell his story on the stage would be if *he* played Christopher and he got everyone else to play their parts for real!'[5]

Christopher-as-director tells one actor that he is 'too old' to play the role of a policeman and is cross when he does so anyway (83; 87); corrects actors' entrances and exits (96); and orders that the action be replayed if the actors don't play the scenes exactly how he wrote them. When Christopher has arrived at his mother's flat, for example, and Roger and Judy are giving him breakfast, he interrupts the action to contradict the actor playing Roger: 'It was Mother who gave me the milkshake, not you' (113). The scene is reset: Judy-as-actress picks up the milkshake to give to Christopher, who informs her that 'you need to shout more loudly at him. Like you're really angry with him not just being nice' (113). Judy-as-actress nods, agrees and replays the action – this time with more anger – and looks to Christopher, '*expecting more feedback*' on her performance (113). Judy has clearly got it right this time, as Christopher continues with the narrative: 'I have to go back to Swindon' (113). Apart from the humour derived from Christopher's rather haughty style of directing, this moment emphasizes the fact that the play we are watching is *his* story: we are in his world and these are his rules.

Language

As previously discussed, Christopher's mind is extremely literal and his use of language reflects this. He very rarely uses figurative language and avoids colloquialisms and slang. Unlike the adults around him, he never swears. He speaks in full sentences and even takes pains to pronounce most words in full, rather than abbreviating or contracting two words together (he will typically say 'do not' rather than 'don't'). The resulting formality of Christopher's

5 Luke Treadaway, telephone interview with Jacqueline Bolton, 14 July 2015.

conversation is undercut only by his habit of speaking in long sentences, connecting separate clauses by the conjunctions 'and', 'but' and 'so'. While his sentences are often over-long, however, his use of grammar and syntax (the order of words in a sentence) is always correct. He typically speaks in factual statements and, when questioned, will reply with all the information required to provide the fullest possible answer.

With the exception of Siobhan, the language used by the adults around Christopher is far more casual and colloquial. Ed, in particular, frequently uses slang and everyday figurative expressions such as 'Jesus wept', 'Every Tom, Dick and Harry' and 'lose my rag' – phrases which are alien to Christopher unless he has deliberately learnt their culturally-acquired meanings (he has learned that 'chow' means 'food', for example [69]). In contrast to Christopher, whose excellent command of language means that he can confidently articulate himself, Ed Boone lacks the confidence to work through his problems verbally. He swears easily and often and when trying to explain himself – as when he discovers Christopher with the letters – he often stutters and has trouble connecting or finishing sentences: 'Oh shit. Oh Christ . . . It was an accident. I don't know what to say . . . I was in such a mess . . .' (77). Expletives (swear words) pepper the speech of most of the adult characters in the play, even those in positions of authority, such as the policemen Christopher encounters. The hostility of this kind of language contributes to the play's implied sense that the world is an aggressive, frightening place from which, in some respects, Christopher is right to withdraw.

Set and lighting design

As already noted, *Curious Incident* is composed of long sequences of short scenes which jump around in both place and time. A detailed set design that tried to realize all these different locations naturalistically would entail lengthy scene changes that would ruin the pace and atmosphere of the play. As Marianne Elliott, director of the 2012 National Theatre production explains, the show's creative team was:

> really clear that we needed to have short, sharp scene changes. To the point where the actors are leaving the stage

> as the next set [of actors] come on – because that's the speed at which Christopher thinks, his brain is faster than any of ours. So Judy can still be walking off [stage], thinking about Polperro, and suddenly Ed's come in because that's where Christopher's head is.[6]

'Marianne's principle concern', confirms Adrian Sutton, composer of the music for *Curious Incident*:

> was that everything had to be played from Christopher's point of view. So, in terms of scenic design, everything had to be very ordered, very exact and precise. The same went for the lighting and the movement – in fact, every element of the stagecraft of that play is lined up like iron filings pointing in that direction, in Christopher's ability to control and understand what's around him.[7]

Bunny Christie's set design seated the audience on four edges of a square playing space, the floor of which resembled mathematical graph paper: white lines forming a glowing grid of tiny squares on a black background. The floor was a blackboard, onto which Christopher could chalk emoticons and diagrams as he tried to deduce Wellington's killer. This space became a virtual map of Christopher's mind, revealing his inner life through lighting and video projections of whirling algebraic equations, galaxies of stars and cascading numbers and letters. Choreography by Scott Graham and Steven Hoggett of physical theatre company Frantic Assembly created gymnastic dance-like sequences which vividly dramatized Christopher's physical, mental and emotional journey through the play. Everything required to tell Christopher's story – props, costumes and, most importantly, the ensemble of actors themselves – remained visible onstage throughout and the only pieces of set were eight portable boxes ingeniously configured by the ensemble to evoke the play's various locations, including Christopher's street, a train carriage and a luggage rack. Where specific locations remained necessarily abstract, this was complemented by a specific focus on

6 Marianne Elliott, telephone interview with Jacqueline Bolton, 19 August 2015.

7 Adrian Sutton, interview with Jacqueline Bolton, London, 24 July 2015.

detail: props were minimal but these, too, worked to convey a sense of Christopher's own unique perception of the world, as Elliott explains:

> Christopher doesn't really like eye contact, so when talking to somebody he would fixate on a particular object that that character might be holding, like garden shears, or an oven glove. So it felt important that that object was the only prop in the scene and that it was a very bright colour because, for him, it's of heightened importance, it's what he's fixating on.

The aim of the production, states Elliott, was to enable 'the audience to feel what Christopher feels emotionally, even though he never articulates emotion – to get inside how he feels about missing his mum in the first half, or inside the hell of that journey in the second half'. Critics who attended the press night of the 2012 National Theatre production were unanimous in their praise for the production's design: 'evoking the strange algebra of Christopher's thought processes', wrote one critic, '[the production] allows us to see him as if from the inside'.[8]

Things to remember

A play is not only a creative work of fiction, it is also *a set of instructions for performance*. When you read a play, you are not only asked to imagine characters and a story, you are also invited to imagine the theatrical event itself. When reading a play, you will notice that there are two different types of writing on the page: the *dialogue* spoken by characters and the *stage directions* which provide more information about what the characters do, how the dialogue should be spoken and where the scene takes place. While there is a limit as to how much of the play's visual, aural and physical dimensions a play-text can record, if you wish to enter into the playwright's imagination you must read *both* the dialogue and the stage directions to try and visualize how the play might look, sound and feel on a stage.

8 Henry Hitchings, *The Curious Incident of the Dog in the Night-Time* review, *Evening Standard*, 3 August 2012.

Things to do

Stephens describes the way Christopher thinks as 'balletic':

> The agility with which he moves from thought to thought is the agility of a dancer. [The production was] an attempt to dramatize [. . .] the interior of Christopher Boone's brain. [I wanted] to get what's *in* there *outside* in his behaviour.[9]

- In a group, discuss what production strategies you would use to 'dramatize the interior of Christopher Boone's brain'. You might like to think about aspects such as music, choreography, lighting, video projection, sound, and set design.

9 Simon Stephens, Theatre Talk, 'The Curious Incident with [sic] the Dog in the Night-Time', 12 November 2014: <https://www.youtube.com/watch?v=3sHa5Zr_iYU> [Accessed 20 August 2015].

The Curious Incident of the Dog in the Night-Time

The Curious Incident of the Dog in the Night-Time received its world premiere at the National Theatre's Cottesloe Theatre, 2 August 2012, with the following cast and creative team:

Christopher Boone	Luke Treadaway
Siobhan	Niamh Cusack
Ed	Paul Ritter
Judy	Nicola Walker
Mrs Alexander	Una Stubbs
Mrs Shears	Sophie Duval
Mr Thompson	Matthew Barker
No. 40 Rhiannon	Harper-Rafferty
Roger Shears	Nick Sidi
Reverend Peters	Howard Ward

All other parts played by members of the Company

Director Marianne Elliott
Designer Bunny Christie
Lighting Designer Paule Constable
Video Designer Finn Ross
Movement Directors Scott Graham and Steven Hoggett for Frantic Assembly
Music Adrian Sutton
Sound Designer Ian Dickinson for Autograph
Associate Director Nadia Fall
Fight Director Kate Waters
Resident Director Katy Rudd

Characters

Christopher
Siobhan
Ed, *Christopher's dad*
Mrs Alexander
Judy, *Christopher's mother*
Mrs Shears / Voice One / Mrs Gascoyne / Woman on Train / Woman on Heath
Policeman One / Voice Two / Mr Thompson / Rhodri / Man behind Counter / Posh Man / Drunk Two / Shopkeeper / Roger
Duty Sergeant / Voice Three / Mr Wise / Uncle Terry / Drunk One / London Transport Policeman / Customer / Man on Phone
Reverend Peters / Voice Four / Station Policeman / Ticket Collector / Station Guard / Man with Socks / London Policeman / Ukrainian One
Number 44 / Voice Five / Lady in Street / Information / Punk Girl / Ukrainian Two

All actors remain on stage unless prescribed otherwise.

There is also a dead dog. With a fork sticking out of it.

Scenes run into one another without interruption regardless of alterations in space or time or chronology.

Part One

A dead dog lies in the middle of the stage. A large garden fork is sticking out of its side.

Christopher Boone, *fifteen years old, stands on one side of it. His forty-two-year-old neighbour* **Mrs Shears** *stands on the other.*

They stand for a while without saying anything. The rest of the company watch, waiting to see who is going to dare to speak first.

Mrs Shears What in Christ's name have you done to my dog?

Christopher *is frozen to the spot.*

Mrs Shears Oh no. Oh no. Oh no. Oh Christ.

Christopher's *teacher, twenty-seven-year-old* **Siobhan** *opens* **Christopher**'s *book. She reads from it.*

Siobhan It was seven minutes after midnight. The dog was lying on the grass in the middle of the lawn in front of Mrs Shears' house.

Mrs Shears Get away from my dog.

Siobhan Its eyes were closed. It looked as if it was running on its side, the way dogs run when they think they are chasing a cat in a dream. But the dog was not running or asleep. The dog was dead.

Mrs Shears Get away from my dog.

Siobhan There was a garden fork sticking out of the dog. The dog was called Wellington. It belonged to Mrs Shears who was our friend. She lived on the opposite side of the road, two houses to the left.

Mrs Shears Get away from my dog.

Christopher *takes two steps away from the dog.*

Siobhan My name is Christopher John Francis Boone. I know all the countries of the world and the capital cities. And every prime number up to 7507.[1]

Mrs Shears Get away from my dog, for Christ's sake.

Christopher *puts his hands over his ears. He closes his eyes. He rolls forward. He presses his forehead on to the grass. He starts groaning.*

Siobhan After twelve and a half minutes a policeman arrived. He had a big orange leaf stuck to the bottom of his shoe which was poking out from one side. This is good, Christopher. It's quite exciting. I like the details. They make it more realistic.

A **Policeman** *enters. He has a big orange leaf stuck to the bottom of his shoe, which is poking out to one side. He squats next to* **Christopher**.

Siobhan He squatted down next to me. He said to me:

Policeman One Would you like to tell me what's going on here, young man?

Christopher *stops groaning.*

There is some time.

Christopher *lifts his head from the ground.*

There is some time.

Christopher *looks at the* **Policeman**.

There is some time.

Siobhan I do not tell lies. Mother used to say that this was because I was a good person. But it is not because I am a good person. It is because I can't tell lies.

Christopher The dog is dead.

Policeman One I'd got that far.

1 A prime number is a number that is only divisible by 1 and itself.

Christopher I think someone killed the dog.

Policeman One How old are you?

Christopher I'm fifteen years and three months and two days.

Policeman One And what precisely are you doing in the garden?

Christopher I'm talking to you.

Policeman One Why were you in the garden in the first place?

Christopher I could see Wellington in the garden, it looked like someone tried to plant him.[1]

Policeman One Did you try to plant the dog?

Christopher No, I did not. I like dogs.

Policeman One Did you kill the dog?

Christopher I did not kill the dog.

Policeman One Is this your fork?

Christopher No.

Policeman One You seem very upset about this.

I'm going to ask you once again.

Christopher *starts groaning*.

Policeman One Terrific.

Christopher *carries on groaning*.

Policeman One Young man I'm going to ask you to stop making that noise and to stand up please calmly and quietly.

Christopher *carries on groaning*.

Policeman One Marvellous. Great. Just flipping –

1 This is a slight play on words for the audience. You can 'plant' a tree, bush or flower (remember Christopher and the Policeman are in a garden) but you can also 'plant' evidence – that is, deliberately place something incriminating (something which suggests the guilt of someone) for later discovery.

The **Policeman** *tries to lift him up by his arm.*

Christopher *screams. He hits the* **Policeman**.

The **Policeman** *stares at* **Christopher**. *For a while the two look at one another, neither entirely sure what to say or quite believing what has just happened.*

Policeman One I'm arresting you for assaulting a police officer.

I strongly advise you to get into the back of the police car because if you try any of that monkey-business again, you little shit, I am going to seriously lose my rag. Is that understood?

Siobhan I find people confusing. This is for two main reasons. The first main reason is that people do a lot of talking without using any words. Siobhan says that if you raise one eyebrow it can mean lots of different things. It can mean 'I want to do sex with you'. I never said that.

Christopher Yes you did.

Siobhan I didn't use those words, Christopher.

Christopher You did on September 12th last year. At first break.

Siobhan And it can also mean 'I think that what you just said was very stupid'.

Duty Sergeant Could you take your laces out of your shoes please, Christopher?

He does.

Thank you. Could you empty your pockets on to the desk please?

Christopher Is that in case I have anything in them that I could use to kill myself or escape or attack a policeman with?

The **Duty Sergeant** *looks at him for a beat.*

Duty Sergeant That's right.

Christopher I've got a Swiss Army knife but I only use that for doing odd jobs not for stabbing things or hurting people.

Duty Sergeant Jolly good.

Voice Four A piece of string.

Voice Five A piece of a wooden puzzle.

Voice Six Three pellets of rat food for Toby, my rat.

Voice One £1.47 (this was made up of a £1 coin, a 20p coin, two 10p coins, a 5p coin and a 2p coin).

Voice Six A red paperclip.

Voice Four A key for the front door.

Voice Five A Swiss Army knife with thirteen attachments including a wire stripper and a saw and a toothpick and tweezers.

Christopher *empties his pockets.*

Duty Sergeant Could you take your watch off please, Christopher?

Christopher No.

Duty Sergeant I'm sorry, Christopher?

Christopher I need my watch to know exactly what time it is.

Duty Sergeant Take your watch off please, Christopher.

Christopher, please will you take your watch off. I'm asking you for a final time.

Give it here, lad.

The **Duty Sergeant** *tries to take the watch.*

Christopher *starts screaming.*

The **Duty Sergeant** *stops. He moves away. He nods his head.* **Christopher** *stops screaming.*

Duty Sergeant It's all right, son. You keep it.

Christopher *calms down.*

Duty Sergeant Do you have any family, Christopher?

Christopher Yes I do.

Duty Sergeant And who is your family?

Christopher Father and Mother but Mother's dead. And also Uncle Terry who is in Sunderland. He is my father's brother and my grandparents too but three of them are dead and Grandma Burton is in a home because she has senile dementia and thinks I'm someone on television.[1]

Duty Sergeant Right. Lovely. Do you know your father's phone number, Christopher?

Christopher *turns to* **Ed. Ed** *looks at him. He holds his hand out in front of him with his fingers stretched.*

Christopher *does the same. They touch fingers.*

Then let go.

Christopher I could see the Milky Way as we drove towards the town centre.

Ed Could you?

Christopher Some people think the Milky Way is a long line of stars, but it isn't. Our galaxy is a huge disc of stars of millions of light years across and the solar system is somewhere near the outer edge of the disc.[2]

Ed *says nothing.*

1 Dementia describes a set of symptoms that may include memory loss and difficulties with language. It is most commonly caused by Alzheimer's, which is a physical disease of the brain. Senile Dementia was a term used when it was thought that memory loss and confusion was simply a normal part of ageing, rather than being caused by a specific brain disease. These days it is referred to simply as 'dementia'.

2 The Universe contains billions of galaxies. A galaxy is a system of stars, gas, dust and dark matter, bound together by gravity. The Milky Way is the galaxy that contains the Earth's Solar System. The Solar System comprises the Sun and the planetary system that orbits it (Mercury, Venus, Earth, Mars, Jupiter, Saturn, Uranus and Neptune).

Christopher For a long time scientists were puzzled by the fact that the sky is dark at night even though there are billions of stars in the universe and there must be stars in every direction you look, so that the sky should be full of starlight because there is very little in the way to stop the light reaching earth.

Ed *stares at him. Says nothing.*

Christopher Then they worked out that the universe was expanding, that the stars were all rushing away from one another after the Big Bang and the further the stars were away from us the faster they were moving, some of them nearly as fast as the speed of light, which was why their light never reached us.[1]

Ed Is that right?

Christopher And when the universe has finished exploding all the stars will slow down, like a ball that has been thrown into the air and they will come to a halt and they will all begin to fall towards the centre of the universe again. And then there will be nothing to stop us seeing all the stars in the world because they will all be moving towards us, gradually faster and faster and we will know that the world is going to end soon because when we look up into the sky at night there will be no darkness, just the blazing light of billions and billions of stars, all falling.

Ed Terrific.

Duty Sergeant Christopher. Mr Boone. Could you come this way please?

Christopher Are you going to interview me and record the interview?

Duty Sergeant I don't think there will be any need for that.

1 The Big Bang theory states that about 13.7 billion years ago all the matter in the Universe was concentrated into an extremely hot and dense single point, which expanded rapidly in a hot explosion and is still expanding today. After the initial expansion, the universe cooled sufficiently to allow the formation of atoms, which later came together to form stars and galaxies. The speed of light is the maximum speed at which all matter and information in the universe can travel. It takes about eight minutes and seventeen seconds for the light from the sun to reach earth, which is an approximate distance of 150,000,000 kilometres.

I've spoken to your father and he says you didn't mean to hit the policeman.

Did you mean to hit the policeman?

Christopher Yes.

Duty Sergeant But you didn't mean to hurt the policeman?

Christopher No. I didn't mean to hurt the policeman, I just wanted him to stop touching me.

Duty Sergeant You know that it's wrong to hit a policeman don't you?

Christopher I do.

Duty Sergeant Did you kill the dog, Christopher?

Christopher I didn't kill the dog.

Duty Sergeant Do you know that it is wrong to lie to a policeman and that you can get into a very great deal of trouble if you do?

Christopher Yes.

Duty Sergeant Do you know who killed the dog?

Christopher No.

Duty Sergeant Are you telling the truth?

Christopher Yes. I always tell the truth.

Duty Sergeant Right. I'm going to give you a caution.

Christopher Is that going to be on a piece of paper like a certificate I can keep?

Duty Sergeant No. A caution means that we are going to keep a record of what you did, that you hit a policeman but that it was an accident and that you didn't mean to hurt the policeman.

Christopher But it wasn't an accident.

Ed Christopher, please.

Duty Sergeant If you get into any more trouble we will take out this record and see that you have been given a caution and we will take things much more seriously. Do you understand what I'm saying?

Christopher Yes.

Siobhan The second main reason is that people often talk using metaphors. These are examples of metaphors:

Voice One I am going to seriously lose my rag.

Voice Two He was the apple of her eye.

Voice Three They had a skeleton in the cupboard.

Voice Four We had a real pig of a day.

Voice Five The dog was stone dead.

Siobhan The word metaphor means carrying something from one place to another and it is when you describe something by using a word for something that it isn't. This means that the word metaphor is a metaphor. Sorry? This means that the word metaphor is a metaphor. Wow. That's clever.

Christopher It's true.

Siobhan Yes. I think it should be called a lie because a pig is not like a day and people do not have skeletons in their cupboards. And when I try and make a picture of the phrase in my head it just confuses me because imagining an apple in someone's eye doesn't have anything to do with liking someone a lot and it makes you forget what the person was talking about.

Christopher *turns to* **Ed.**

Christopher I'm sorry.

Ed It's OK.

Christopher I didn't kill the dog.

Ed I know.

Christopher, you have to stay out of trouble, OK?

Christopher I didn't know I was going to get into trouble. I like Wellington and I went to say hello to him, but I didn't know that someone had killed him.

Ed Just try and keep your nose out of other people's business.

Christopher I am going to find out who killed Wellington.

Ed Were you listening to what I was saying, Christopher?

Christopher Yes, I was listening to what you were saying but when someone gets murdered you have to find out who did it so that they then can be punished.

Ed It's a bloody dog, Christopher, a bloody dog.

Christopher I think dogs are important too.

Ed Leave it.

Christopher I wonder if the police will find out who killed him and punish the person.

Ed I said leave it, for God's sake.

Christopher Are you sad about Wellington?

Ed Yes, Christopher, you could say that. You could very well say that.

Siobhan *reads more from the book.*

Siobhan Mother died two years ago.

I came home from school one day and no one answered the door, so I went and found the secret key that we keep under a flowerpot outside the kitchen window. I let myself into the house and wiped my feet on the mat. I put my keys in the bowl on the table. I took my coat off and hung by the side of the fridge so it would be ready for school the next day and gave three pellets of rat food to Toby who is my pet rat. I made myself a raspberry milkshake and heated it up in the microwave. Then I went up to my bedroom and turned on my bedroom light and played six games of Tetris and got to level 38 which is my fourth best ever score.[1] An hour later Father came home from work.

Ed Christopher, have you seen your mum?

Christopher No.

Siobhan He went downstairs and started making some phone calls. I did not hear what he said. Then he came up to my room and said he had to go out for a while and he wasn't sure how long he would be. He said that if I needed anything I should call him on his mobile phone.

Some of the company look at **Siobhan** *or* **Christopher** *or* **Ed** *waiting to find out what happens next.*

Siobhan He was away for two and a half hours. When he came back I went downstairs.

Other characters watch **Christopher** *as he approaches* **Ed**.

Ed *doesn't look at* **Christopher**. *There is some time before* **Ed** *speaks.*

Ed I'm afraid you won't be seeing your mother for a while.

Christopher Why not?

Ed Your mother has had to go into hospital.

Christopher Can we visit her?

Ed No.

Christopher Why can't we?

Ed She needs rest. She needs to be on her own.

Christopher Is it a psychiatric hospital?

Ed No. It's an ordinary hospital. She has a problem . . . a problem with her heart.

1 Tetris is a tile-matching puzzle video game. Its popularity soared in the 1990s following the launch of a handheld version for the Nintendo Game Boy.

Christopher We will need to take food to her.

Ed I'll take some to her during the day when you're at school and I'll give it to the doctors and they can give it to your mum, OK?

Christopher But you can't cook.

Ed Christopher. Look. I'll buy some ready-made stuff from Marks and Spencer's and take those in. She likes those.

Christopher I'll make her a get-well card.

If I make her a get-well card will you take it in for her tomorrow?

Siobhan How are you today, Christopher?

Christopher I'm very well, thank you.

Siobhan That's good.

Christopher In the bus on the way to school we passed four red cars in a row.[1]

Siobhan Four?

Christopher So today is a Good Day.

Siobhan Great. I am glad.

Christopher I've decided I am going to try and find out who killed Wellington because a Good Day is a day for projects and planning things.

Siobhan Who's Wellington?

Christopher Wellington is a dog that used to belong to my neighbour Mrs Shears who is our friend but he is dead now because somebody killed him by putting a garden fork through

1 In Haddon's novel, Christopher elaborates on his system: '4 red cars in a row made it a **Good Day**, and 3 red cars in a row made it a **Quite Good Day**, and 5 red cars in a row made it a **Super Good Day**, and [. . .] 4 yellow cars in a row made it a **Black Day**, which is a day when I don't speak to anyone and sit on my own reading books and don't eat my lunch and *Take No Risks*'.

him. And I found him and then a policeman thought I'd killed him but I hadn't and then he tried to touch me so I hit him and then I had to go to the police station.

Siobhan Gosh.

Christopher And I am going to find out who really killed Wellington and make it a project. Even though Father told me not to.

Siobhan Did he?

Christopher Yes.

Siobhan I see.

Christopher I don't always do what I'm told.

Siobhan Why?

Christopher Because when people tell you what to do it is usually confusing and does not make sense. For example, people often say 'Be quiet' but they don't tell you how long to be quiet for.

Siobhan No. Why did your father tell you not to try to find out who killed Wellington, Christopher?

Christopher I don't know.

Siobhan Christopher, if your father's told you not to do something maybe you shouldn't do it.

Well, we're meant to be writing stories today, so why don't you write about what happened to you last night?

Christopher OK I will.

Siobhan I can help you.

Christopher Will you help me with the spelling and the grammar and the footnotes?[1]

1 A footnote is an additional piece of information – usually a reference or a comment – placed at the bottom of a page. What you are reading now is a footnote! Footnotes do not usually feature in novels but Christopher's concern to include them reflects his love of order, detail and precision.

Ed Christopher, I'm sorry, your mother's died.

She's had a heart attack.

It wasn't expected.

Christopher What kind of heart attack?

Ed I don't know what kind of heart attack. Now isn't the moment, Christopher, to be asking questions like that.

Christopher It was probably an aneurysm.[1]

Ed I'm sorry, Christopher, I'm really sorry.

A form representing Christopher's street is assembled.

Siobhan That evening I went round to Mrs Shears' house and knocked on the door and waited for her to answer it.

Mrs Shears *answers her door. She is drinking a cup of tea.*

Mrs Shears What are you doing here?

Christopher I wanted to come and tell you that I didn't kill Wellington. And also I want to find out who killed him.

Mrs Shears Christopher, I really don't think I want to see you right now.

Christopher Do you know who killed Wellington?

Mrs Shears Can you go now, Christopher.

Christopher I wanted to see if the fork was in the shed.

Mrs Shears If you don't go now I will call the police again.

Christopher Reverend Peters, where is heaven?

Reverend Peters I'm sorry, Christopher?

1 An aneurysm is like a blood-filled balloon lodged in the wall of a blood vessel. If an aneurysm ruptures it can lead to death.

Christopher In our universe whereabouts is it exactly?

Reverend Peters It's not in our universe. It's another kind of place altogether.

Christopher There isn't anything outside our universe, Reverend Peters. There isn't another kind of place altogether. Except there might be if you go through a Black Hole.[1] But a Black Hole is what is called a Singularity which means it's impossible to find out what is on the other side because the gravity of a Black Hole is so big that even electromagnetic waves like light can't get out of it, and electromagnetic waves are how we get information about things which are far away. And if heaven is on the other side of a Black Hole then dead people would have to be fired into space on a rocket to get there and they aren't or people would notice.

Reverend Peters *looks at him for a while before he responds.*

Reverend Peters Well when I say heaven is outside our universe it's really just a manner of speaking. I suppose what it really means is that they are with God.

Christopher But where is God?

Reverend Peters Christopher, we should talk about this on another day when I have more time.

Siobhan The next day was Saturday and there is not much to do on a Saturday unless Father takes me out somewhere on an outing to the boating lake or to the garden centre, but on this Saturday England were playing Romania at football which meant that we weren't going to go on an outing because Father wanted to watch the match on the television. So I made a decision. I decided to do some more detection.[2] I decided to go out on my own.

Mr Thompson Can I help you?

1 A black hole is a region of space which exerts such a powerful gravitational pull that nothing – including light – can escape from inside it.

2 Christopher is playing at being a detective, like his hero Sherlock Holmes.

Christopher Do you know who killed Wellington?

Mr Thompson Who are you?

Christopher I'm Christopher Boone from number 36 and I know you. You're Mr Thompson.

Mr Thompson I'm Mr Thompson's brother.

Christopher Do you know who killed Wellington?

Mr Thompson Who the hell is Wellington?

Christopher Mrs Shears' dog. Mrs Shears is from number 41.

Mr Thompson Someone killed her dog?

Christopher With a fork.

Mr Thompson Jesus Christ.

Christopher A garden fork. Do you know who killed him?

Mr Thompson I haven't a bloody clue.

Christopher Did you see anything suspicious on Thursday evening?

Mr Thompson Look son, do you really think you should be going round asking questions like this?

Christopher Yes, because I want to find out who killed Wellington and I am writing a book about it.

Mr Thompson Well, I was in Colchester on Thursday so you're asking the wrong bloke.

Christopher Thank you.

Number 44 It's Christopher isn't it?

Christopher Yes it is. Do you know who killed Wellington?

Number 44 No. No. I don't. No. I'm sorry.

Christopher Did you see anything suspicious on Thursday evening, which might be a clue?

Number 44 Like what?

Christopher Like strangers or the sound of people arguing.

Number 44 I didn't, Christopher, no.

Christopher Do you know of anyone who might want to make Mrs Shears sad?

Number 44 Perhaps you should be talking to your father about this.

Christopher I can't talk to my father about it because he told me to stay out of other people's business.

Number 44 Well maybe he has a point, Christopher.

Christopher So you don't know anything that might be a clue?

Number 44 No. You be careful, young man.

Christopher I will be. Thank you for helping me with my questions.

Do you know who killed Wellington on Thursday night?

Mr Wise Bloody hell. Policemen really are getting younger, aren't they?[1]

Mr Wise *laughs*. **Christopher** *walks away*.

Christopher Do you know anything about Wellington getting killed?

Mrs Alexander I'm afraid you're going to have to say that again. I'm a little deaf.

Christopher Do you know anything about Wellington getting killed?

Mrs Alexander I heard about it yesterday. Dreadful. Dreadful.

Christopher Do you know who killed him?

1 That 'policemen are getting younger' is a commonplace observation usually uttered by adults who recognize (or, indeed, *do not* recognize!) that in fact it is *they* who are getting *older*. Mr Wise is making a joke about Christopher's age but Christopher, who is unable to understand humour, does not realize this and dislikes being laughed at.

Mrs Alexander No, I don't.

Christopher Somebody must know because the person who killed Wellington knows that they killed Wellington. Unless they were a mad person and didn't know what they were doing. Or unless they had amnesia.[1]

Mrs Alexander Well, I suppose you're probably right.

Christopher Thank you for helping me with my investigation.

Mrs Alexander You're Christopher, aren't you?

Christopher Yes. I live at number 36.

Mrs Alexander We haven't talked before, have we?

Christopher No. I don't talk to strangers. But I'm doing detective work.

Mrs Alexander I see you every day, going to school. It's very nice of you to come and say hello. Even if it's only because you're doing detective work.

Christopher Thank you.

Mrs Alexander I have a grandson your age.

Christopher My age is fifteen years and three months and three days.

Mrs Alexander Well, almost your age. You don't have a dog, do you?

Christopher No.

Mrs Alexander You'd probably like a dog, wouldn't you?

Christopher I have a rat.

Mrs Alexander A rat?

Christopher He's called Toby.

Mrs Alexander Oh.

1 Amnesia is the medical term to describe memory loss caused by damage to the brain.

Christopher Most people don't like rats because they think they carry diseases like bubonic plague.[1] But that's only because they lived in sewers and stowed away on ships coming from foreign countries where there were strange diseases. But rats are very clean.

Mrs Alexander Do you want to come in for tea?

Christopher I don't go into other people's houses.

Mrs Alexander Well maybe I could bring some tea out here. Do you like lemon squash?

Christopher I only like orange squash.

Mrs Alexander Luckily I have some of that as well. And what about Battenberg?

Christopher I don't know because I don't know what Battenberg is.

Mrs Alexander It's a kind of cake. It has marzipan icing round the edge.

Christopher Is it a long cake with a square cross-section which is divided into equally sized, alternately coloured squares.

Mrs Alexander Yes, I think you could probably describe it like that.

Christopher I think I'd like the pink squares but not the yellow squares because I don't like yellow. And I don't know what marzipan is so I don't know whether I'll like that.

Mrs Alexander I'm afraid marzipan is yellow too. Perhaps I should bring out some biscuits instead. Do you like biscuits?

Christopher Yes. Some sorts of biscuits.

Mrs Alexander I'll get a selection.

She goes into her house.

1 Bubonic plague is the most common form of plague in humans. Black rats were blamed for the bubonic plague (also known as 'the Black Death') that swept through Asia, Europe and African in the fourteenth century, killing an estimated fifty million people, but it was the infected fleas they were carrying which in fact spread the disease.

He waits. Then before she gets back.

Siobhan She moved very slowly because she was an old lady and she was inside the house for more than six minutes and I began to get nervous because I didn't know her well enough to know whether she was telling the truth about getting orange squash and Battenberg cake. And I thought she might be ringing the police and then I'd get into much more serious trouble because of the caution. So I walked away.

Christopher Why would you kill a dog?

Siobhan I wouldn't.

Christopher I think you would only kill a dog if (a) you hated the dog or (b) if you were mad or (c) because you wanted to make Mrs Shears upset. I don't know anybody who hated Wellington so if it was (a) it was probably a stranger. I don't know any mad people either, so if it was (b) it was also probably a stranger.

Siobhan Right.

Christopher But most murders are committed by someone who is known to the victim. In fact, you are most likely to be murdered by a member of your own family on Christmas Day.

Siobhan Is that a fact?

Christopher Yes actually it is a fact. Wellington was therefore most likely to have been killed by someone known to him. I only know one person who didn't like Mrs Shears and that is Mr Shears who divorced Mrs Shears and left her to live somewhere else and who knew Wellington very well indeed. This means that Mr Shears is my Prime Suspect.[1]

1 The prime suspect of an investigation is the individual that the police believe most probably committed the crime. Christopher loves to use vocabulary associated with detective fiction and his delight in this terminology is indicated in the text by capitalizing the first letter of both words.

Siobhan Christopher.

Christopher I am going to find out more about Mr Shears.

Mrs Gascoyne Mr Boone, nobody has ever taken an A-Level in the school before.

Ed He can be the first then.

Mrs Gascoyne I don't know if we have the facilities in the school to allow him to do that.

Ed Then get the facilities.

Mrs Gascoyne I can't treat Christopher differently to any other student.

Ed Why not?

Mrs Gascoyne Because then everybody would want to be treated differently.

Ed So?

Mrs Gascoyne It would set a precedent. Christopher can always do his A-Levels later. When he's eighteen.

Ed Christopher is getting a crap enough deal already, don't you think, without you shitting on him from a great height as well. Jesus, this is the one thing he's really good at.

Mrs Gascoyne We should talk about this later. Maybe on our own.

Ed Are there things which you're too embarrassed to say to me in front of Christopher?

Mrs Gascoyne No. It's not that.

Ed Say them now then.

Mrs Gascoyne If Christopher sits an A-Level then he would have to have a member of staff looking after him on his own in a separate room.

Ed I'll pay for it. They can do it after school. Here. Fifty quid. Is that enough?

Mrs Gascoyne Mr Boone.

Ed I'm not going to take no for an answer.

Ed *turns to* **Christopher**.

Ed Where have you been?

Christopher I have been out.

Ed I have just had a phone call from Mrs Shears. What the hell were you doing poking round her garden?

Christopher I was doing detective work trying to figure out who killed Wellington.

Ed How many times do I have to tell you, Christopher? I told you to keep your nose out of other people's business.

Christopher I think Mr Shears probably killed Wellington.

Ed (*shouts*) I will not have that man's name mentioned in my house.

Beat.

Everybody on stage pauses to look at **Ed** *and* **Christopher**.

Christopher Why not?

Ed That man is evil.

Christopher Does that mean he might have killed Wellington?

Ed Jesus wept.[1]

Christopher I know you told me not to get involved in other people's business but Mrs Shears is a friend of ours.

Ed Well, she's not a friend any more.

1 A phrase commonly used to express frustration. It comes from a story in the Bible's New Testament in which Jesus weeps at the death of a friend (John 11:35).

Christopher Why not?

Ed OK Christopher. I am going to say this for the last and final time. I will not tell you again. Look at me when I'm talking to you, for God's sake. Look at me. You are not to go asking Mrs Shears who killed that bloody dog. You are not to go asking anyone who killed that bloody dog. You are not to go trespassing on other people's gardens. You are to stop this ridiculous bloody detective game right now. I am going to make you promise me, Christopher. And you know what it means when I make you promise.

Christopher I know.

Ed Promise me that you will give up this ridiculous game right now, OK?

Christopher I promise.

Siobhan I think I would make a very good astronaut.

Ed Yes mate. You probably would.

Siobhan To be a good astronaut you have to be intelligent and I'm intelligent. You also have to understand how machines work and I'm good at understanding how machines work.

Christopher You also have to be someone who would like being on their own in a tiny spacecraft thousands and thousands of miles away from the surface of the earth and not panic or get claustrophobia or homesick or insane.[1] And I really like little spaces so long as there is no one else in them with me.

Ed I noticed.

Siobhan Sometimes when I want to be on my own I get into the airing cupboard and slide in beside the boiler and pull the door closed behind me and sit there and think for hours and it makes me feel very calm.

Christopher So I would have to be an astronaut on my own or have my own part of the spacecraft that no one else could come

1 Claustrophobia is the fear of being in small spaces.

into. And also there are no yellow things or brown things in a spacecraft so that would be OK, too.

And I would have to talk to other people from Mission Control, but we would do that through a radio link-up and a TV monitor so it wouldn't be like real people who are strangers but it would be like playing a computer game.[1]

Ed Which you like.

Christopher Also I wouldn't be homesick at all because I'd be surrounded by lots of things I like, which are machines and computers and outer space. And I would be able to look out of a little window in the spacecraft and know that there was no one else near me for thousands and thousands –

Ed Christopher.

Christopher What?

Ed Could you please, just, give it a bit of a break, mate. Please.

The two look at each other.

Siobhan And know that there was no one else near me for thousands and thousands of miles which is what I sometimes pretend at night in the summer when I go and lie on the lawn and look up at the sky and I put my hands round the sides of my face so that I can't see the fence and the chimney and the washing line and I can pretend I'm in space.

And all I could see would be stars. And stars are the places where the molecules that life is made of were constructed billions of years ago. For example, all the iron in your blood, which stops you being anaemic, was made in a star.

And I would like it if I could take Toby with me into space, and that might be allowed because they sometimes do take animals into space for experiments, so if I could think of a good experiment you

1 Mission Control refers to the large flight control team of highly trained engineers and technicians who monitor and direct human spaceflights, from point of lift-off to the end of the mission.

could do with a rat that didn't hurt the rat, I could make them let me take Toby.

But if they didn't let me I would still go because it would be a Dream Come True.

Christopher Father said.

Siobhan I see, that's a pity.

Christopher So the book is finished.

Siobhan Well, Christopher, if your father said he wanted you to stop then I think he probably has a good reason and I think you should stop. But you can still be very proud because what you've written so far is just, well it's great.

Christopher It's very short.

Siobhan Well, some very good books are very short.

Christopher Like what?

Siobhan Like, like *Heart of Darkness*.

Christopher Who wrote *Heart of Darkness*?

Siobhan Joseph Conrad.

Christopher Did you like my diagram of the universe?

Siobhan I did. Very much.

Christopher And the map of the street. Which is accurate. And the way the chapters are all prime numbers.[1]

Siobhan I noticed that.

Christopher It's not a proper book.

Siobhan Why not?

1 These features of Christopher's book were included Haddon's original novel.

Christopher It doesn't have a proper ending. I never found out who killed Wellington. So the murderer is still At Large.[1]

Siobhan Not all murders are solved, Christopher. Not all murderers are caught.

Christopher I don't like the idea that he could be living somewhere nearby and that I might meet him when I go out for a walk at night.

Siobhan I don't think that's going to happen, Christopher.

Christopher It could do. Murder is usually committed by a person known to the victim.

Father said I was never to mention Mr Shears' name in our house again and that he was an evil man and maybe that meant he was the person who killed Wellington.

Siobhan Christopher, I think you should do what your father tells you to do.

Mrs Alexander What happened to you the other day?

Christopher Which day?

Mrs Alexander I came out again and you'd gone. I had to eat all the biscuits myself.

Christopher I went away.

Mrs Alexander I gathered that.

Christopher I thought you might ring the police.

Mrs Alexander Why on earth would I do that?

Christopher Because I was poking my nose into other people's business and Father said I shouldn't investigate who killed Wellington. And a policeman gave me a caution and if I get into trouble again it will be a lot worse because of the caution.

1 This is another instance of Christopher using the language of law enforcement.

Mrs Alexander You're very shy aren't you, Christopher?

Christopher I'm not allowed to talk to you.

Mrs Alexander Don't worry, I'm not going to tell the police and I'm not going to tell your father because there's nothing wrong with having a chat. Having a chat is just being friendly, isn't it?

Christopher I don't do chatting.

Mrs Alexander Do you like computers?

Christopher Yes. I like computers. I have a computer at home in my bedroom.

Mrs Alexander I know. I can see you sitting at your computer in your bedroom sometimes when I look across the street.

Christopher And I like maths and looking after Toby. And I also like outer space and I like being on my own.

Mrs Alexander I bet you're very good at maths, aren't you?

Christopher I am. I'm going to do A-Level Maths next month. And I'm going to get an A grade.

Mrs Alexander Really? A-Level Maths?

Christopher Yes. I don't tell lies.

Mrs Alexander I apologize. I didn't mean to suggest that you were lying. I just wondered if I heard you correctly. I'm a little deaf sometimes.

Christopher I remember you told me. I'm the first person to do an A-Level from my school because it's a special school.[1]

Mrs Alexander Well, I am very impressed. And I hope you do get an A.

Christopher I will.

1 Christopher here indicates that he attends a non-mainstream school for children and young adults with learning disabilities.

Mrs Alexander And the other thing I know about you is your favourite colour is not yellow.

Christopher No. And it's not brown either. My favourite colour is red. And metal colour. Do you know Mr Shears?

Mrs Alexander Not really, no. I mean I knew him well enough to say hello and talk to a little in the street, but I didn't know much about him. I think he worked in a bank. The National Westminster in town.

Christopher I don't know where that is.

Mrs Alexander It's by the train station.

Christopher I don't know where the train station is either because I don't like to go anywhere outside unless I'm on the school bus to school.

Mrs Alexander Yes, I know how you feel.

Christopher Father said that he is an evil man. Do you know why he said that? Is Mr Shears an evil man?

Mrs Alexander Why are you asking me about Mr Shears, Christopher? Is this about Wellington? Perhaps it would be best not to talk about these things, Christopher.

Christopher Why not?

Mrs Alexander Because. Because maybe your father is right and you shouldn't go round asking questions about this.

Christopher Why?

Mrs Alexander Because obviously he is going to find it quite upsetting.

Christopher Why is he going to find it quite upsetting?

Mrs Alexander Because . . . because I think you know why your father doesn't like Mr Shears very much.

Christopher Did Mr Shears kill Mother?

Mrs Alexander Kill her?

Christopher Yes. Did he kill Mother?

Mrs Alexander No. No. Of course he didn't kill your mother.

Christopher But did he give her stress so that she died of a heart attack?

Mrs Alexander I honestly don't know what you're talking about, Christopher.

Christopher Or did he hurt her so that she had to go into hospital?

Mrs Alexander Did she have to go into hospital?

Christopher Yes. And it wasn't very serious at first but she had a heart attack when she was in hospital.

Mrs Alexander Oh my goodness.

Christopher And she died.

Mrs Alexander Oh my goodness. Oh Christopher, I am so, so sorry. I never realized.

Christopher Why did you say 'I think you know why your father doesn't like Mr Shears very much'?

Mrs Alexander Oh dear, dear, dear. So you don't know?

Christopher Don't know what?

Mrs Alexander Christopher look, I probably shouldn't be telling you this. Perhaps we should take a little walk in the park together. This is not the place to be talking about this kind of thing.

Ed *starts watching their conversation.*

Mrs Alexander I am going to say something to you and you must promise not to tell your father that I told you this.

Christopher Why?

Mrs Alexander I shouldn't have said what I said. And if I don't explain, you'll carry on wondering what I meant. And you might ask your father. And I don't want you to do that because I don't want you to upset him. So I'm going to explain why I said what I said. But before I do that you have to promise not to tell anyone I said this to you.

Christopher Why?

Mrs Alexander Christopher, please, just trust me.

Christopher I promise.

Mrs Alexander Your mother before she died was very good friends with Mr Shears.

Christopher I know.

Mrs Alexander No Christopher, I'm not sure that you do. I mean that they were very good friends. Very, very good friends.

Christopher Do you mean that they were doing sex?

Mrs Alexander Yes, Christopher. That is what I mean.

I'm sorry, Christopher. I really didn't mean to say anything that was going to upset you. But I wanted to explain. Why I said what I said. You see I thought you knew. That's why your father thinks Mr Shears is an evil man. And that will be why he doesn't want you going around talking to people about Mr Shears. Because that will bring back bad memories.

Christopher Was that why Mr Shears left Mrs Shears, because he was doing sex with someone else when he was married to Mrs Shears?

Mrs Alexander Yes. I expect so. I'm sorry, Christopher. I really am.

Christopher I think I should go now.

Mrs Alexander Are you OK, Christopher?

Christopher I can't be on my own with you because you are a stranger.

Mrs Alexander I'm not a stranger, Christopher, I'm a friend.

Ed And what have you been up to, young man?

Christopher I went to the shop to get some liquorice laces and a Milky Bar.

Ed You were a long time.

Christopher I talked to Mrs Alexander's dog outside the shop.

Rhodri God you do get the third degree, don't you? So how are you doing, captain?

Christopher I'm doing very well, thank you, Rhodri.

Rhodri What's 251 times 864?

Christopher 216,864. Is that right?

Rhodri I haven't got a bloody clue.

Ed I'll stick one of these Gobi Aloo Sag things in the oven for you, OK?

Christopher OK.

Rhodri With your little bottle of red paint in it, eh Christopher?[1]

Christopher It's not red paint, it's red food colouring because I don't eat yellow food. If you put red paint into a curry it would be extremely dangerous and it would probably kill you.

Siobhan Have you told your father about this?

Christopher No.

Siobhan Are you going to tell your father about this?

Christopher No.

1 Ed offers to heat up a microwave meal for Christopher's dinner. Gobi Aloo Sag is an Indian dish of cauliflower with potato and spinach. As both cauliflower and potato are 'yellow' coloured, and Christopher dislikes the colour yellow, he adds red food colouring to the dish. It is interesting to note that it is not the taste or texture of 'yellow' food that Christopher dislikes, simply the colour itself.

Ed *goes to* **Siobhan**.

He looks at her holding the book.

He reaches his hand out for it.

After a short time she passes it to him.

He finds the place she was at.

He begins reading **Christopher***'s book.*

Siobhan Did it make you sad to find this out?

Christopher Find what out?

Siobhan Did it make you sad to find out that your mother and Mr Shears had an affair?

Christopher No.

Siobhan Are you telling the truth, Christopher?

Christopher I always tell the truth. I don't feel sad about it because Mother is dead and because Mr Shears isn't around any more. So I would be feeling sad about something that isn't real and doesn't exist and that would be stupid.

Siobhan What was your mother like, Christopher?

Do you remember much about her?

Christopher I remember the 4th of July 2006. I was nine years old. It was a Saturday. We were on holiday in Cornwall. We were on the beach in a place called Polperro. Mother was wearing a pair of shorts made out of denim and a light blue bikini top and she was smoking cigarettes called Consulate, which were mint flavour. And she wasn't swimming. She was sunbathing on a towel, which had red and purple stripes, and she was reading a book by Georgette Heyer called *The Masqueraders*. And then she finished sunbathing and went into the water and she said

Judy Bloody Nora, it's cold.

Christopher (*simultaneously*) 'Bloody Nora, it's cold.' And she said I should come and swim too, but I didn't like swimming because I don't like taking my clothes off. And she said I should just roll up my trousers and walk into the water a little way. So I did. And Mother said

Judy Look, it's lovely.

Christopher And she jumped backwards and disappeared under the water and I thought a shark had eaten her and I screamed. And she stood up out of the water again and came over to where I was standing and held up her right hand and spread out her fingers like a fan.

Judy Come on, Christopher, touch my hand. Come on now. Stop screaming. Touch my hand. Listen to me, Christopher. You can do it. It's OK, Christopher. It's OK. There aren't any sharks in Cornwall.

Ed 'When we were inside the park Mrs Alexander stopped walking and said "I am going to say something to you and you must promise not to tell your father that I told you this".'

Christopher And other times she used to say

Judy If I hadn't married your father I think I'd be living in a little farmhouse in the South of France with someone called Jean. And he'd be, ooh, a local handyman. You know, doing painting and decorating for people, gardening, building fences. And we'd have a veranda[1] with figs growing over it and there would be a field of sunflowers at the bottom of the garden and a little town on the hill in the distance and we'd sit outside in the evening and drink red wine and smoke Gauloise cigarettes and watch the sun go down.

Ed What is this?

Christopher *looks at* **Ed**.

Christopher It's a book I'm writing.

Ed Is this true? Did you speak to Mrs Alexander?

1 A veranda is an open-air porch, a semi-sheltered space ideal for sitting in in warm weather. Judy is painting a rosy picture of rustic luxury.

Christopher Yes.

Ed Jesus, Christopher, how stupid are you? What the hell did I tell you, Christopher?

Christopher Not to mention Mr Shears name in the house. And not to go asking Mrs Shears, or anyone, about who killed that bloody dog. And not to go trespassing on other people's gardens. And to stop this bloody ridiculous detective game. Except I haven't done any of those things. I just asked Mrs Alexander about Mr Shears because . . .

Ed Don't give me that bollocks, you little shit. You knew exactly what you were bloody doing. I've read the book, remember. What else did I say, Christopher?

Christopher I don't know.

Ed Come on, you're the memory man. Not to go round sticking your nose into other people's business. And what do you do? You go around sticking your nose into other people's business. You go around raking up the past and sharing it with every Tom, Dick and Harry you bump into.[1] What am I going to do with you, Christopher? What am I going to do with you, Christopher?

Christopher I was just chatting with Mrs Alexander. I wasn't doing investigating.

Ed I ask you to do one thing for me, Christopher. One thing.

Christopher I didn't want to talk to Mrs. Alexander. It was Mrs Alexander who . . .

Ed *grabs* **Christopher***'s arm.*

Christopher *screams.*

Ed *shakes* **Christopher** *hard with both hands.*

Christopher *punches* **Ed** *repeatedly in the face. He cuts his mouth.*

Ed *hits the side of* **Christopher***'s head.*

1 'Every Tom, Dick and Harry' is a colloquial phrase meaning 'anybody and everybody'.

Christopher *falls unconscious for a few seconds.*

Ed *stands above him. He is still holding the book.*

Ed I need a drink.

He leaves.

He comes back without the book. He looks at **Christopher** *for a while before he speaks.*

Everybody else on stage watches what he says.

Ed I'm sorry I hit you.

I didn't mean to.

I love you very much, Christopher. Don't ever forget that. I know I lose my rag occasionally.[1] And I know I shouldn't. But I only do it because I worry about you, because I don't want to see you getting into trouble, because I don't want you to get hurt. Do you understand?

Christopher Where's my book?

Ed Christopher, do you understand that I love you?

Ed *holds his right hand up and spreads his fingers out in a fan.*

Christopher *does the same with his left hand.*

They make their fingers and thumbs touch each other.

Christopher Is it in the dustbin at the front of the house?

Siobhan Christopher, why have you got a bruise on the side of your face?

Christopher Father was angry. He grabbed me so I hit him and then we had a fight.

Siobhan Did he hit you?

1 To 'lose your rag' is a colloquial expression meaning to lose your temper.

Christopher I don't know. I got very cross. It made my memory go strange.

Siobhan Did he hit you because he was angry?

Christopher He didn't hit me. He grabbed me. But he was angry.

Siobhan Did he grab you hard?

Christopher Yes.

Siobhan Christopher, are you frightened of going home?

Christopher No. Because I need to find my book.

Siobhan Do you want to talk about it any more?

Christopher No. Because grabbing is OK if it's on your arm or your shoulder when you are angry, but you can't grab someone's hair or their face. But hitting is not allowed, except if you are already in a fight with someone then it is not so bad.

Siobhan When I got home from school Father was still at work so I went outside and looked inside the dustbin.

But the book wasn't there.

I wondered if Father had put it into his van and driven to the tip and put it into one of the big bins there but I did not want that to be true because then I would never see it again. One other possibility was that Father had hidden my book somewhere in the house. So I decided to do some detecting and see if I could find it.

I started by looking in the kitchen.

Then I detected in the utility room.[1]

Then I detected in the dining room.

1 Christopher has resumed his 'detective game'. Christopher's use of the verb 'to detect' here is unusual and indicative of both his idiosyncratic manner of speaking and his love of detective fiction.

Then I detected in the living room where I found the missing wheel from my Airfix Messerschmitt Bf 109 G-6 model under the sofa.

Then I went upstairs but I didn't do any detecting in my own room because I reasoned that Father wouldn't hide something from me in my own room unless he was being very clever and doing what is called a Double Bluff like in a real murder mystery novel, so I decided to look in my own room only if I couldn't find the book anywhere else.[1]

I detected in the bathroom, but the only place to look was in the airing cupboard and there was nothing in there.

Which meant the only room left to detect in was Father's bedroom.

I started by looking under the bed.

There were seven shoes and a comb with lots of hair in it and a piece of copper pipe and a chocolate biscuit and a magazine called *Fiesta*[2] and a dead bee and a Homer Simpson pattern tie and a wooden spoon, but not my book. Then I looked in the drawers on either side of the dressing table.

But these only contained aspirin and nail clippers and batteries and dental floss and a tampon and tissues and a spare false tooth but my book wasn't there either.

Then I looked in his clothes cupboard. In the bottom of the cupboard was a large plastic toolbox which was full of tools for doing-it-yourself but I could see these without opening the box because it was made of transparent grey plastic. Then I saw that there was another box underneath the toolbox.

So I lifted the toolbox out of the cupboard.

1 The Cambridge English Dictionary defines a double bluff as: 'a clever attempt to deceive someone, especially by telling that person the truth when they think you are telling lies'. To hide Christopher's book in Christopher's own room would be a double bluff because Christopher would never think of searching his own room to find something that was being deliberately hidden from him. Ed, however, has not been that clever.

2 *Fiesta* is a British soft-core pornographic magazine. Dubbed as 'the magazine for men which women love to read', it was Britain's top selling adult magazine in the 1970s.

The other box was an old cardboard box that is called a shirt box because people used to buy shirts in them.

Christopher *finds these things including, finally the shirt box.*

Siobhan And when I opened the shirt box I saw my book was inside it.

Christopher *finds his book.*

Siobhan Then I heard his van pulling up outside the house and I knew that I had to think fast and be clever.

I heard Father shutting the door of the van.

And that is when I saw the envelope.

It was an envelope addressed to me and it was lying under my book in the shirt box with some other envelopes. I picked it up.

Christopher *finds the envelope.*

Siobhan It had never been opened.

It said

Judy Christopher Boone, 36 Randolph Street, Swindon, Wiltshire.

Siobhan Then I noticed there were lots of envelopes and they were all addressed to me. And this was interesting and confusing.

And then I noticed how the words 'Christopher' and 'Swindon' were written. They were written like this.

Judy Christopher. Swindon.

Siobhan I only know three people who do little circles instead of dots over the letter i. And one of them is Siobhan. And one of them was Mr Loxley who used to teach at the school. And one of them was Mother.

Ed Christopher?

Christopher Hello.

Ed So what have you been up to, young man?

Christopher Today we did Life Skills with Siobhan. Which was Using Money and Public Transport. And I had tomato soup for lunch and three apples. And I practised some maths in the afternoon and we went for a walk in the park with Mrs Peters and collected leaves for making collages.

Ed Excellent, excellent. What do you fancy for chow tonight?[1]

Christopher Baked beans and broccoli.

Ed I think that can be very easily arranged.

I'm just going to put those shelves up in the living room if that's all right with you. I'll make a bit of a racket,[2] I'm afraid, so if you want to watch television we're going to have to shift it upstairs.

Christopher I'll go and be on my own in my room.

Ed Good man.

Siobhan I went up to my room. And when I was in the room I shut the door and took out the envelope. I opened the envelope. Inside there was a letter. And this was what was written in the letter.

Judy 451c Chapter Road, Willesden, London NW2 5NG. 0208 887 8907. Dear Christopher. I'm sorry it's been such a very long time since I wrote my last letter to you. I've been very busy. I've got a new job working as a secretary for a factory that makes things out of steel. You'd like it a lot. The factory is full of huge machines that make the steel and cut it and bend it into whatever shapes they need. Also we've moved into a new flat at last as you can see from the address. It's not as nice as the old one and I don't like Willesden very much, but it's easier for Roger to get to work and he's bought it (he only rented the other one) so we can get our own furniture and paint the walls the colour we want to. You haven't written to me yet, so I know that you are probably still angry with me. I'm sorry, Christopher. But I still love you. I hope you don't stay angry with me for ever. And I'd love it if you were able to write me a letter (but remember to send it to the new address!).

1 'Chow' is an informal word for food; here, dinner.
2 'To make a racket' is a colloquial way of saying 'to make a lot of noise'.

I think about you all the time.

Lots of love,

Your Mum.

Siobhan I was really confused. Mother had never worked as a secretary for a firm that made things out of steel. And Mother had never lived in London. And Mother had never written a letter to me before.

There was no date on the letter so I couldn't work out when Mother had written the letter and then I looked at the front of the envelope and I saw there was a postmark and there was a date on the postmark which meant that the letter was posted eighteen months after Mother had died.

Ed What are you doing?

Christopher I'm reading a letter.

Ed I've finished the drilling. That David Attenborough nature programme's on telly if you're interested.

Christopher OK.

Ed *leaves.*

Christopher *watches him go. He looks at the letter. He folds it and puts it back in its envelope and hides it in the box he's sitting on.*

Siobhan When I started writing my book there was only one mystery to solve. Now there were two. Perhaps the letter was in the wrong envelope and it had been written before Mother had died. Perhaps it wasn't a letter from Mother. Perhaps it was a letter to another person called Christopher from that Christopher's mother. Perhaps someone else had written the letter and pretended to be Mother.

I decided that I would not think about it any more that night because I didn't have enough information and could easily LEAP TO THE WRONG CONCLUSIONS.[1]

1 Again, Christopher is using the language of detective fiction.

He lies down. He curls himself up into a ball.

Night falls. Morning rises.

The next day **Christopher** *comes home from school.*

Ed You're soaking.

Christopher Yes.

Ed Give me your coat, I'll hang it up.

How was school?

Christopher It was good, thank you.

Joseph Fleming took his trousers off and went to the toilet all over the floor of the changing room and started to eat it, but Mr Davis stopped him.

Ed Good old Mr Davis eh?

Christopher Joseph eats everything.

Ed Does he?

Christopher He once ate one of the little blocks of blue disinfectant, which hang inside the toilets. And he once ate a £50 note from his mother's wallet. And he eats string and rubber bands and tissues and writing paper and paints and plastic forks. Also he bangs his chin and screams a lot.

Ed I know how he feels. Christopher –

Christopher Tyrone said that there was a horse and a pig in the poo so I said he was being stupid, but Siobhan said he wasn't. They were small plastic animals from the library that the staff use to make people tell stories. And Joseph had eaten them.

Ed Christopher, I've got to go out.

Christopher Why?

Ed I've just had a call. There's a lady. Her cellar has flooded. I've got to go out and fix it.

Christopher Is it an emergency?

Ed Yes mate.

Christopher Why can't Rhodri go?

Ed He's already out on a call.

Christopher So there are two emergencies.

Ed That's right, mate.

Christopher It is raining very heavily.

Ed It is.

Christopher The rain looks like white sparks.

Ed Christopher, if I go out will you be OK?

Christopher Yes I will because there's no one around because everybody's staying indoors.

Ed Good. Good. Good. Good lad.

Christopher I like looking at the rain.

Ed Terrific.

Christopher I like it because it makes me think how all the water in the world is connected.

Ed Does it?

Christopher This water, this rain has evaporated actually from somewhere like maybe the Gulf of Mexico maybe or Baffin Bay and now it's falling in front of the house and it will drain away into the gutter and flow to a sewage station and then it will be cleaned and then it will go into a river and then it will go back into the ocean again.[1]

Ed I'll have my mobile with me.

1 Christopher is here describing the water cycle, the scientific term for which is hydrologic cycle.

Christopher Yes.

Ed So you can call me if there's a problem.

Christopher Yes.

Ed Behave yourself, Christopher yeah?

Christopher Yes.

Ed *remains on stage.*

Siobhan So I went into his bedroom and opened up the cupboard and lifted the toolbox off the top of the shirt box and opened the shirt box. I counted out the letters. There were forty-three of them. They were all addressed to me in the same handwriting. I took one and opened it. Inside was this letter.

As **Judy** *reads so* **Christopher** *begins to assemble his train set. His building becomes frantic. At times almost balletic.*

Judy 451c Chapter Road, London NW2 5NG. 0208 887 8907. I was looking through some old photos last night, which made me sad. Then I found a photo of you playing with the train set we bought for you a couple of Christmases ago. And that made me happy because it was one of the really good times we had together. Do you remember how you played with it all day and you refused to go to bed at night because you were still playing with it? We told you about train timetables and you made a train timetable and you had a clock and you made the train run on time. And there was a little wooden station, too, and we showed you how people who wanted to go on the train went to the station and bought a ticket and then got on a train? And then we got out a map and we showed you the little lines which were the train lines connecting all the stations. And you played with it for weeks and weeks and weeks and we bought you more trains and you knew where they were all going. I liked remembering that a lot.

Siobhan Then I opened another envelope. This was the letter that was inside.

Christopher *continues to build a train set. It should be as big as he can possibly make it. He makes it with attention and detail as the letter continues.*

Judy Dear Christopher. I said that I wanted to explain to you why I went away when I had the time to do it properly. Now I have lots of time. So I'm sitting on the sofa here with this letter and the radio on and I'm going to try and explain.

I was not a very good mother, Christopher. Maybe if things had been different, maybe if you'd been different, I might have been better at it. But that's just the way things turned out.

I'm not like your father. Your father is a much more patient person. He just gets on with things and if things upset him he doesn't let it show.

But that's not the way I am and there's nothing I can do to change it.

Do you remember once when we were shopping in town together? And we went into Bentall's[1] and it was really crowded and we had to get a Christmas present for Grandma? And you were frightened because of all the people in the shop. It was the middle of Christmas shopping when everyone was in town. And I was talking to Mr Land who works on the kitchen floor and went to school with me. And you crouched down on the floor and put your hands over your ears and you were in the way of everyone so I got cross because I don't like shopping at Christmas either, and I told you to behave and I tried to pick you up and move you. But you shouted and you knocked those mixers off the shelf and there was a big crash. And everyone turned round to see what was going on and Mr Land was really nice about it but there were boxes and bits of string and bits of broken bowl on the floor and everyone was staring and I saw that you had wet yourself and I was so cross and I wanted to take you out of the shop but you wouldn't let me touch you and you just lay on the floor and screamed and banged your hands and feet on the floor and the manager came and asked me what the problem was and I was at the end of my tether and I

1 Bentalls is a small chain of up-market English department stores.

had to pay for two broken mixers and we just had to wait until you stopped screaming. And then I had to walk you all the way home, which took hours because I knew you wouldn't go on the bus again.

And I remember that night I just cried and cried and cried and your father was really nice about it at first and he made you supper and put you to bed and he said these things happen and it would be OK. But I said I couldn't take it any more and eventually he got really cross and he told me I was being stupid and said I should pull myself together and I hit him, which was wrong, but I was so upset.

We had a lot of arguments like that.

Because I often thought I couldn't take it any more. And your father is really patient, but I'm not. I get cross, even though I don't mean to. And by the end we stopped talking to each other very much because we knew it would always end up in an argument. And I felt really lonely.

Siobhan And that was when I started spending lots of time with Roger.

Judy And that was when I started spending lots of time with Roger.

Christopher *moves to the middle of the track. He crouches down. He rolls himself into a ball. He starts hitting his hands and his feet and his head against the floor as the letter continues.*

Judy And I know you might not understand any of this, but I wanted to try to explain so that you knew.

Siobhan We had a lot in common. And then we realized that we were in love with one ano –

Judy I said that I couldn't leave you and he was sad about that but he understood that you were really important to me.

Siobhan And you started to shout and I got cross and I threw the food across the room. Which I know I shouldn't have done.

Judy You grabbed the chopping board and you threw it and it hit my foot and broke my toes.

Siobhan And afterwards at home your father and I had a huge argument.

Judy And I couldn't walk properly for a month, do you remember, and your father had to look after you.

Siobhan And I remember looking at the two of you and seeing you together and thinking how you were really different with him. Much calmer.

Judy And it made me so sad because it was like you didn't need me at all.

Siobhan And I think then I realized you and your father were probably better off if I wasn't living in the house.

Judy And Roger asked me if I wanted to come with him.

Siobhan And it broke my heart but eventually I decided it would be better for all of us if I went.

Judy And so I said yes.

Siobhan And I meant to say goodbye.

Judy But when I rang your father he said I couldn't –

He was really angry. He said I couldn't –

Siobhan He said I couldn't talk to you.

Judy And I didn't know what to do.

Siobhan He said I was being selfish and that I was never to set foot inside the house again.

Judy And so I haven't.

Siobhan I wonder if you can understand any of this. I know it will be difficult for you.

Judy I thought what I was doing was the best for all of us. I hope it is.

Siobhan Christopher, I never meant to hurt you.

Judy I used to have dreams that everything would get better. Do you remember you used to say that you wanted to be an astronaut?

Well I used to have dreams where you were an astronaut and you were on television and I thought that's my son. I wonder what it is that you want to be now. Has it changed? Are you still doing maths? I hope you are.

Have you got the present I sent you? Have you solved it yet? Roger and I saw it in a shop in Camden market and I know you've always liked puzzles.

Siobhan Roger tried to get the two pieces apart before we wrapped it up and he couldn't do it.

He said that if you managed it you were a genius.

Judy Loads and loads of love, Mother.

Christopher*'s thrashing has exhausted him.*

He has been sick. He lies still for a while, wrapped in a ball.

The box of his mother's letters is next to him.

Ed Christopher? Christopher?

Christopher *doesn't respond.*

Ed Christopher, what the hell are you doing? These are. Oh shit. Oh Christ.

Christopher *doesn't move or respond.*

Ed *stops himself from crying.*

Ed It was an accident.

Christopher *doesn't respond.*

Ed I don't know what to say . . . I was in such a mess . . . I said she was in hospital. Because I didn't know how to explain, it was so complicated. And once I'd said that . . . I couldn't change it. It just . . . It got out of control.

Christopher *doesn't respond.*

After a time **Ed** *approaches him.*

Very, very gently he touches his shoulder. **Christopher** *doesn't respond.*

Ed Christopher, we have to get you cleaned up, OK?

Let's sit you up and get your clothes off and get you into bed, OK? I'm going to have to touch you, but it's going to be all right.

Ed *lifts* **Christopher** *on to the side of the bed.* **Christopher** *doesn't resist or fight at all.*

Ed *takes* **Christopher***'s jumper and shirt off.*

Siobhan *has entered. She has a tube of Smarties.*

Siobhan Christopher, what do you think is in here?

Christopher Smarties.

She opens it.

Siobhan It's not Smarties. It's a pencil. If your Dad came in now, and we asked him what was inside the Smarties tube, what do you think he would say?

Christopher A pencil.

Ed Have you had anything to eat this evening?

Can I get you anything to eat, Christopher?

OK. Look. I'm going to go and put your clothes into the washing machine and then I'll come back, OK?

Ed *leaves.* **Christopher** *sits alone and counts.*

Christopher 2, 4, 8, 16, 32, 64, 128, 256, 512, 1024, 2048, 4096, 8192, 16384, 32768, 65536, 131072, 262144, 524288, 1048576, 2097152, 4194304, 8388608, 16777216, 33554432.

Ed How are you feeling? Can I get you anything?

Look maybe I shouldn't say this, but . . . I want you to know that you can trust me. Life is difficult, you know. It's bloody hard telling the truth all the time. But I want you to know that I'm trying. And perhaps this is not a very good time to say this, and I know you're not going to like it, but . . . You have to know that I am going to tell you the truth from now on. About everything. Because . . . if you don't tell the truth now, then later on it hurts even more. So . . . I killed Wellington, Christopher. Just . . . let me explain. When your mum left . . . Eileen . . . Mrs Shears . . . she was very good to me. She helped me through a very difficult time. And I'm not sure I would have made it without her. Well, you know how she was round here most days. Popping over to see if we were OK. If we needed anything . . . I thought . . . Well . . . Shit, Christopher, I'm trying to keep this simple . . . I thought she might carry on coming over . . . I thought . . . and maybe I was being stupid . . . I thought she might . . . eventually . . . want to move in here. Or that we might move into her house. We . . . we got on really, really well. I thought we were friends. And I guess I thought wrong. We argued, Christopher, and . . . She said some things I'm not going to say to you because they're not nice, but they hurt, but . . . I think she cared more for that bloody dog than for us. And maybe that's not so stupid, looking back. Maybe it's easier living on your own looking after some stupid mutt than sharing your life with other actual human beings. I mean, shit, buddy we're not exactly low maintenance, are we? Anyway, we had this row. Well, quite a few rows to be honest. But after this particularly nasty little blow-out, she chucked me out of the house. And you know what that bloody dog was like. Nice as pie one moment, roll over, tickle its stomach. Sink its teeth into your leg the next. Anyway, we're yelling at each other and it's in the garden. So when she slams the door behind me the bugger's waiting for me. And . . . I know, I know. Maybe if I'd just given it a kick it would probably have backed off. But, shit Christopher, when the red mist comes down . . . Christ, you know what I'm talking about. I mean we're not that different me and you.[1] And it was like everything I'd been bottling up for two years just . . .

I promise you, I never meant for it to turn out like this.

Ed *holds his right hand up for* **Christopher** *to touch.*

1 'Red mist' is a slang term describing a fit of extreme anger that temporarily clouds a person's judgement. Ed is referring here to the tendency to physically lash out when angry that both he and Christopher share. See Christopher's description to Siobhan of his fight with his father: 'I got very cross. It made my memory go strange' (65).

Christopher *screams.*

He pushes **Ed** *backwards.*

Ed *stares at* **Christopher**.

Ed OK. Look. Christopher. I'm sorry. Let's leave it for tonight, OK? I'm going to go downstairs and you get some sleep and we'll talk in the morning. It's going to be all right. Honestly. Trust me.

Ed *leaves.*

Christopher *fields himself into a ball. He groans.*

He starts counting again.

Christopher 2, 4, 8, 16, 32, 64, 128, 256, 512, 1024, 2048, 4096, 8192, 16384, 32768, 32768, 32768, 32768, 32 –

Siobhan Father had murdered Wellington. That meant he could murder me.

I had to get out of the house.

I had to get out of the house.

I had to get out of the house.

I had to get out of the house.

I had to get out of the house.

I made a decision. I did this by thinking of all the things I could do and deciding whether they were the right decision or not.

Ed Stay home.

Siobhan I decided I couldn't stay home any more.

Ed Christopher, please.

Christopher No, because I can't live in the house with you any more because it is dangerous.

(*To* **Siobhan**.) I can't go and live with you because you can't look after me when school's closed.

Siobhan I could try and –

Christopher No, because you're a teacher.

Siobhan Yes.

Christopher Not a friend or a member of my family.

Uncle Terry You could go and live with your Uncle Terry.

Christopher You live in Sunderland. I don't know how to get to Sunderland.

Uncle Terry Get a train. Get the train from Swindon.

Christopher And you smoke cigarettes. And you stroke my hair.

You're not a friend either.

Mrs Alexander I think I am a friend.

Christopher No. And you're not a member of my family.

Mrs Alexander I do have a dog.

Christopher Yes but I can't stay overnight in your house or use your toilet because you've used it and you're a stranger.

Mrs Alexander I'm not really a stranger, Christopher.

Christopher Yes.

Judy 451c Chapter Road, London NW2 5NG.

451c Chapter Road, London NW2 5NG.

451c Chapter Road, London NW2 5NG.

Christopher *looks at* **Judy**.

Judy 451c Chapter Road.

Christopher London NW2 5NG.

Light falls.

Part Two

The company is on stage.

Siobhan Christopher, I want to ask you something. Mrs Gascoyne has asked if we would like to do a play this year. She asked me to ask everybody if we'd like to make some kind of performance for the school. Everybody could join in and play a part in it.

Mrs Gascoyne I think it would be a good thing for everybody to join in and play a part in.

Siobhan I was wondering if you'd like to make a play out of your book.

Christopher No.

Siobhan I think it could be really good fun, Christopher.

Mrs Gascoyne I think it could be really good fun.

Christopher No. It's a book and it's for me and not everybody, just for me.

Siobhan I know that, Christopher, but I think a lot of people would be interested in what would happen if people took your book and started acting bits out of it.

Christopher No. I don't like acting because it is pretending that something is real when it is not really real at all so it is like a kind of lie.

Siobhan But people like stories, Christopher. Some people find things which are kind of true in things which are made up. You like your Sherlock Holmes stories and you know Sherlock Holmes isn't a real person, don't you?[1]

1 Sherlock Holmes is a fictional detective created in the 1890s by the writer Sir Arthur Conan Doyle. *The Curious Incident of the Dog in the Night-Time* takes its title from a line in a short story featuring this famous detective, 'Silver Blazes' (1892). The text does not make it clear whether or not Christopher is aware that Holmes is not a real person.

I would help you if you were worried about that.

Christopher No.

Reverend Peters I think I'd rather like to take the part of a policeman.

Christopher You're too old to be a policeman.

Ed (*shouting*) Christopher. Christopher.

Everybody stops what they're doing and watches **Ed**.

Christopher *hides.*

Nobody gives **Ed** *a clue as to where* **Christopher** *is.*

After a while he gives up.

Then **Christopher** *comes out. He is holding Toby in his cage.*

Mrs Alexander Christopher, what on earth has happened to you?

Christopher Can you look after Toby for me?

Mrs Alexander Who's Toby?

Christopher Toby's my pet rat.

Mrs Alexander Oh . . . Oh yes. I remember now. You told me.

Christopher He eats special pellets and you can buy them from a pet shop. And he needs new water in his bottle every day, too.

Mrs Alexander Why do you need somebody to look after Toby, Christopher?

Christopher I'm going to London.

Mrs Alexander How long are you going for?

Christopher Until I go to university.

Mrs Alexander Right. Are you and your father moving house?

Christopher No.

Mrs Alexander So, why are you going to London?

Christopher I'm going to live with Mother.

Mrs Alexander I thought you told me your mother was dead.

Christopher I thought she was dead but she was still alive. And Father lied to me. And also he killed Wellington and so that means that he could kill me.

Mrs Alexander Is your mother here?

Christopher No. Mother is in London. She lives at 451c Chapter Road, London NW2 5NG.

Mrs Alexander So you're going to London on your own?

Christopher I think I am going to do that, yes.

Mrs Alexander Look, Christopher, why don't you come inside and sit down and we can talk about this.

Christopher No. I can't come inside. Will you look after Toby for me?

Mrs Alexander I really don't think that would be a good idea, Christopher. Where's your father at the moment, Christopher?

Christopher I don't know.

Mrs Alexander Well perhaps we should try and give him a ring and see if we can get in touch with him. I'm sure he's worried about you. And I'm sure that there's been a dreadful misunderstanding.

Christopher *leaves.*

He goes back to his house.

He sees his dad's wallet on the floor. He stares at it, frozen in his tracks.

He approaches the wallet.

He opens the wallet.

He takes out the card from his dad's wallet. He puts it in his pocket.

Christopher 3558. 3558. 3558. 3558. 3558.[1]

He leaves the house.

The company dismantle the house.

They make Swindon town centre.

Christopher Where can I buy a map?

Lady in Street Pardon?

Christopher Where can I buy a map?

Lady in Street A map of where?

Christopher A map of here.

Lady in Street I don't know, where do you want to get to?

Christopher I'm going to the train station.

Lady in Street You don't need a map to get to the train station.

Christopher I do because I don't know where the train station is.

Lady in Street You can see it from here.

Christopher No I can't. And also I need to know where there is a cash machine.

Lady in Street There. That building. Says 'Signal Point' on the top. There's a British Rail sign on the other end. The station's at the bottom of that.

Christopher Do you mean the stripy building with the horizontal windows that you can see poking out over these houses?

Lady in Street That's the one.

Christopher How do I get to that building?

Lady in Street Gordon Bennett.[2]

1 This is the pin number for Ed's credit card.

2 'Gordon Bennett' is a slang term for an exclamation of surprise, or frustration.

Christopher I knew that the train station was somewhere near. And if something is nearby you can find it by moving in a spiral, walking clockwise and taking every right turn until you come back to a road you've already walked on, then taking the next left, then taking every right turn and so on. And that was how I found the station.

Voice One Customers seeking access to the car park please use assistance phone opposite, right of the ticket office.

Voice Two Warning CCTV in operation.

Voice Three Great Western.

Voice Five Cold beers and lagers.

Voice Two CAUTION WET FLOOR.

Voice Four Your 50p will keep a premature baby alive for 1.8 seconds.

Voice Three Transforming travel.

Voice Five Refreshingly Different.

Voice One It's Delicious, it's creamy and it's only £1.30. Hot Choc Deluxe.

Voice Two 0870 777 7676.

Voice Four The Lemon Tree.

Voice One No Smoking.

Voice Two Fine teas.

Voice Five Automatic Fire Door Keep Clear.

Voice Two Air Conditioned.

Voice Three Reserved Parking.

Voice Four Open As Usual This Way.

Voice Three No Smoking.

Voice Five No alcohol.

Voice Three Dogs must be carried.

Voice One RVP.

Voice Three Dogs must be carried.

Voice One LFB.

Voice Four A Perfect Blend.

Voice Two Royal Mail.

Voice Four Mon-Fri 7 am – 7 pm.

Voice Three Dogs must be carried at all times.

Voice Five Special Lunch Offers.

Voice One Parking Subject to the Railway Bylaws Section 219 of the Transport Act 2000.

Voice Three Please stand on the right.

Voice Four Superb Coffee.

Voice Two Step-free Access.

Voice Five Take Extra Care with Children.

Voice Four Superb Coffee.

Voice Three Cash Dispensers.

Voice Four Superb Coffee.

Voice Three Dogs must be carried at all times.[1]

Station Policeman Are you all right, young man?

Christopher You're too old.

Station Policeman Are you all right, young man?

Christopher You're too old to play a policeman.

1 This section of text voices the visual noise of adverts, signs, notices, brand names, telephone numbers, warnings and posters that Christopher finds at Swindon train station. In performance, this list produces a stream of cacophonous noise which reflects Christopher's sensation of being overwhelmed and disorientated.

Station Policeman Are you all right, young man?

Christopher No.

Station Policeman You're looking a bit worse for wear. The lady at the café says that when she tried talking to you, you were in a complete trance. What's your name?

Christopher Christopher Boone.

Station Policeman Where do you live?

Christopher 36 Randolph Street.

Station Policeman What are you doing here?

Christopher I needed to sit down and be quiet and think.

Station Policeman OK let's keep it simple. What are you doing at the railway station?

Christopher I'm going to see Mother.

Station Policeman Mother?

Christopher Yes, Mother.

Station Policeman When's your train?

Christopher I don't know. She lives in London. I don't know when there's a train to London.

Station Policeman So, you don't live with your mother?

Christopher No. But I'm going to.

Station Policeman So where does your mother live?

Christopher In London.

Station Policeman Yes, but where in London?

Christopher 451c Chapter Road, London NW2 5NG.

Station Policeman Jesus. What is that?

Christopher That's my pet rat, Toby.

Station Policeman A pet rat?

Christopher Yes, a pet rat. He's very clean and he hasn't got bubonic plague.

Station Policeman Well, that's reassuring.

Christopher Yes.

Station Policeman Have you got a ticket?

Christopher No.

Station Policeman So how precisely were you going to get to London then?

Christopher I have a cashpoint card.

Station Policeman Is this your card?

Christopher No, it's Father's.

Station Policeman Father's.

Christopher Yes, Father's.

Station Policeman OK.

Christopher He told me the number. It's 3558.

Station Policeman Why don't you and I take a stroll to the cash machine, eh?

Christopher You mustn't touch me.

Station Policeman Why would I want to touch you?

Christopher I don't know.

Station Policeman Well, neither do I.

Christopher Because I got a caution for hitting a policeman but I didn't mean to hurt him and if I do it again I'll get into even bigger trouble.

Voice One Please insert your card.

Station Policeman You're serious, aren't you?

Christopher Yes.

Voice One Enter your personal number.

Station Policeman You lead the way.

Christopher Where?

Station Policeman Back by the ticket office.

Voice One Please enter amount. Ten pounds. Twenty pounds. Fifty pounds. One hundred pounds.

Christopher How much does it cost to get a ticket to London?

Station Policeman About twenty quid.

Voice One Please wait. Your transaction is being processed.

Christopher Is that pounds?

Station Policeman Christ alive. Yep. It's twenty pounds.

Voice One Please take your card and wait for your cash.

Beat.

Station Policeman Well I guess I shouldn't keep you chatting any longer.

Christopher Where do I get a ticket for the train from?

Station Policeman You are a prize specimen, aren't you?

Christopher Where do I get a ticket for the train from?

Station Policeman In there. Now are you sure you know what you're doing?

Christopher Yes. I'm going to London to live with my mother.

Station Policeman Has your mother got a telephone number?

Christopher Yes.

Station Policeman And can you tell me what it is?

Christopher Yes. It's 020 887 8907.

Station Policeman And you'll ring her if you get into any trouble, OK?

Christopher I want to go to London.

Man behind Counter If you don't mind.

Christopher I want to go to London.

Man behind Counter Single or return?

Christopher What does 'single or return' mean?

Man behind Counter Do you want to go one way or do you want to come back?

Christopher I want to stay there when I get there.

Man behind Counter For how long?

Christopher Until I go to university.

Man behind Counter Single then. That'll be £17.

Christopher When is the train to London?

Man behind Counter Platform One, five minutes.

Christopher Where is Platform One?

Man behind Counter Through the underpass and up the stairs. You'll see the signs.

Siobhan Underpass means tunnel, Christopher.

Somebody bumps into **Christopher**. *He barks at them like a dog.*

Siobhan In your head imagine a big red line across the floor. It starts at your feet and goes through the tunnel. And walk along the line. And count the rhythm in your head because that helps, doesn't it? Like when you're doing music or when you're doing drumming. Left, right, left, right, left, right.

Christopher Left, right, left, right, left, right.

Siobhan See the sign saying Platform One. See the glass door. Go through the glass door, Christopher.

Somebody bumps into **Christopher** *again. Again he barks like a dog.*

Whole Company Watch where the hell you're going.

Siobhan Watch that man. There. See where he presses the button. And the doors slide open.

You do that.

Press the button.

Step through the doors.

Christopher Is this the train to London?

Station Policeman Christopher. Caught you. Just in time. We've got your father at the police station. He's looking for you.

Christopher I know.

Station Policeman So why are you going to London?

Christopher Because I'm going to live with Mother.

Station Policeman Well, I think your father might have something to say about that.

Christopher *tries to run. The* **Policeman** *grabs him.*

Christopher *screams. The* **Policeman** *lets go.*

Station Policeman OK, let's not get over-excited here. I'm going to take you back to the police station and you and me and your dad can sit down and have a little chat about who's going where.

Christopher Have you arrested Father?

Station Policeman Arrested him? What for?

Christopher He killed a dog. With a garden fork. The dog was called Wellington.

Station Policeman Well, we can talk about that as well. Right now, young man, I think you've done enough adventuring for one day.

The **Policeman** *reaches out to touch him. He screams.*

Now listen, you little monkey. You can either do what I say, or I'm going to have to make . . .

The train begins to move.

Bollocks.

Christopher Why are you swearing? Have we started? Has the train started?

Station Policeman Don't move.

Rob? Yeah it's Nigel. I'm stuck here on the bloody train. Yeah. Don't even. . . Look. It stops at Didcot Parkway. So if you can get someone to meet me with a car. . . Cheers. Tell his old man we've got him but it's going to take a while, OK? Great. Let's get ourselves a seat. Park yourself. You are a bloody handful you are. Jeez.

The company rebuild and extend and develop the interior of the train. Including the luggage rack.

Christopher I see everything. Most other people are lazy. They never look at everything. They do what is called glancing, which is the same word for bumping off something and carrying on in almost the same direction. And the information in their head is really simple. For example, if they are on a train looking out of a window at the countryside it might be

Voice One 1. I am sitting on a train looking out at a field that is full of grass.

Voice Two 2. There are some cows in the field.

Voice Three 3. It is sunny with a few clouds.

Voice Four 4. There are some flowers in the grass.

Voice Five 5. There is a village in the distance.

Voice One 6. There is a fence at the edge of the field and it has a gate in.

Christopher And then they would stop noticing anything because they would be thinking something else like

Voice Two Oh it is very beautiful here.

Christopher Or

Voice One I'm worried that I might have left the gas cooker on.

Christopher Or

Voice Four I wonder if Julie has given birth yet.

Christopher But if I am standing looking out of the window of a train on to the countryside I notice everything. Like

As **Christopher** *talks he raps out a nervous rhythm with his hand.*

1. There are nineteen cows in the field. Fifteen of which are black and white and four of which are brown and white.

2. There is a village in the distance, which has thirty-one visible houses and a church with a square tower and not a spire.

3. There are ridges in the field which means that in medieval times it was called a ridge and furrow field and people who lived in the village would have a ridge each to do farming on.

4. There is an old plastic bag from Asda in the hedge and a squashed Coca Cola can with a snail on, and a long piece of orange string.

5. The north-east corner of the field is highest and the south-west corner is lowest.

6. I can see three different types of grass and two colours of flowers in the grass.

7. The cows are mostly facing uphill,

And there were thirty-one more things in this list of things.

Station Policeman Oh Christ, you've wet yourself. For God's sake, go to the bloody toilet, will you?

Christopher But I'm on a train.

Station Policeman They do have toilets on trains, you know.

Christopher Where is the toilet on the train?

Station Policeman Through those doors there. But I'll be keeping an eye on you, you understand?

Christopher No.

Station Policeman Just go to the bloody toilet.

Christopher *stands.*

He walks down the corridor of the train. Shaking, closing his eyes, he pisses.

He tries to wash his hand but can't because there is no running water.

He spits on his hands to wash them. He rubs them dry with toilet paper.

Shaking he leaves the toilet.

He goes to the luggage rack.

He moves two bags.

He climbs on to the shelf.

He hides himself behind the suitcases.

He starts listing prime numbers to himself.

As he continues to count the **Policeman** *notices he's gone. The counting continues under the following exchanges.*

Christopher 2, 3, 5, 7, 11, 13, 17, 19, 23, 29, 31, 37, 41, 43, 47, 53, 59, 61, 67, 71, 73, 79, 83, 89, 97, 101, 103, 107, 109, 113, 127, 131, 137, 139, 149, 151, 157, 163, 167, 173, 179, 181, 191, 193, 197, 199, 211, 223, 227, 229, 233, 239, 241, 251, 257, 263, 269, 271, 277, 281.

Station Policeman Christopher? Christopher? Bloody hell.

He leaves. **Christopher** *stays where he is. Still counting. A woman approaches him to take her bag.*

Woman on Train You scared the living daylights out of me. I think someone's out there on the platform looking for you.

Christopher I know.

Woman on Train Well. It's your look-out.

She takes her bag. She leaves. **Christopher** *stays hidden behind the smaller pile of bags. Still counting. A* **Posh Man** *approaches. He takes his bag.*

Posh Man Have you touched my bag?

Christopher Yes.

He leaves. **Christopher** *stays hidden behind the still smaller pile of bags. Still counting. Two* **Drunk Men** *approach to take their bags.*

Drunk One Come and look at this, Barry. They've got like, a train elf.

Drunk Two Well, we have both been drinking.

Drunk One Perhaps we should feed him some nuts.

Drunk Two You're the one who's bloody nuts.

Drunk One Come on, shift it, you daft bugger. I need more beers before I sober up.

Christopher *is revealed now. He stops counting. He lies still for a while. Then very tentatively he gets down.*

He looks around. For the first time he is alone on stage.

Christopher I waited for nine more minutes but nobody else came past and the train was really quiet. And I didn't move again. So I realized that the train had stopped. And I knew that the last stop on the train was London.

I heard the sound of feet and it was a policeman.

The **Station Policeman** *enters and explores the back of the stage.*

Christopher Not the one who was on the train before.

The **Station Policeman** *looks at* **Christopher**. *Exits, disappointed. Is replaced by a* **London Transport Policeman.**

Christopher And I could see him through the door, in the next carriage, and he was looking under the seats. I decided I didn't like policemen so much any more. So I got off the train.

Christopher *kneels down.*

He rests his head on the ground.

He groans.

Siobhan *comes back on to the stage.* **Christopher** *notices her. He stops groaning.*

The two look at one another for a while.

Siobhan Left right left right left right. Left right left right left right. Left right left right left right.

He smiles at her. He joins in with her. Eventually he carries on without her.

Christopher Left right left right left right left right left right left right left right left right left right left right left right.

A **Ticket Collector** *stops him.*

Ticket Collector I think someone's looking for you, sonny.

Christopher Who's looking for me?

Ticket Collector A policeman.

Christopher I know.

Ticket Collector Oh right. You wait here, and I'll go and tell them.

The **Ticket Collector** *walks off.* **Christopher** *carries on.*

As he walks he counts left and right.

Christopher Left, right, left, right, left, right.

Voice One Sweet Pastries.

Voice Two Heathrow Airport Check-In Here.

Voice One Bagel factory.

Voice Five Eat.

Voice Three Excellence and taste.

Voice Four Yo! Sushi.

Voice One Stationlink.

Voice Two Buses.

Voice Five WH Smith.

Voice Four Mezzanine.

Voice One Heathrow Express.

Voice Two Clinique.

Voice Three First-Class Lounge.

Voice Four Fullers.

Voice Five EasyCar.co.

Voice Two The Mad Bishop.

Voice Three And Bear Public House.

Voice Four Fuller's London Pride.

Voice One Dixons.

Voice Two Our Price.

Voice Three Paddington Bear at Paddington Station.

Voice Five Tickets.

Voice One Taxis.

Voice Two First Aid.

Voice Four Eastbourne Terrace.

Voice Two Way Out.

Voice One Praed Street.

Voice Five The Lawn.

Voice Three Q Here Please.

Voice Four Upper Crust.

Voice One Sainsbury's.

Voice Five Local information.

Voice Three Great Western First.

Voice One Position Closed.

Voice Two Closed.

Voice Four Position Closed.

Voice Three Sock Shop.

Voice Four Fast Ticket Point.

Voice Five Millie's Cookies.

Voice One Coffee.

Voice Two Fergie to Stay at Manchester United.

Voice Three Freshly Baked Cookies and Muffins.

Voice Two Cold Drinks.

Voice Four Penalty Fares.

Voice One Warning.

Voice Three Savoury Pastries.

Voice Four Platform 14.

Voice Five Burger King.

Voice Two Fresh Filled.

Voice Three The Reef Café Bar.

Voice Four Business Travel.

Voice One Special Edition.

Voice Two Top 75 Albums.

Voice Five *Evening Standard.*[1]

As the chorus becomes more cacophonous **Christopher** *finds it more difficult to continue to walk.*

1 These are all adverts, notices, brand names and newspapers that Christopher sees at Paddington Station.

He stops. Rests his head against a box. Puts his hands over his ears.

A **Station Guard** *approaches him.*

Station Guard You look lost.

Christopher *pulls out his Swiss Army knife.*

The **Guard** *backs away.*

Station Guard Whoa, whoa, whoa, whoa.

Christopher *carries on.*

Christopher Left right left right left right left right.

He makes his hand into a telescope to limit his field of vision.

He approaches an information counter.

Is this London?

Is this London?

Information Sure is, honey.

Christopher Is this London?

Information Indeed it is.

Christopher How do I get to 451c Chapter Road, London NW2 5NG?

Information Where is that?

Christopher It's 451c Chapter Road, London, NW2 5NG. And sometimes you can write it 451c Chapter Road, Willesden, London NW2 5NG.

Information Take the tube to Willesden Junction. Or Willesden Green. Got to be near there somewhere.

Christopher What sort of tube?

Information Are you for real? Over there. See that big staircase with the escalators? See the sign? Says Underground. Take the Bakerloo Line to Willesden Junction or the Jubilee to Willesden Green. You OK, honey?

Ed Don't do this, Christopher.

Christopher Get away from me.

Ed Christopher, you won't be able to.

Christopher I'm doing really well.

Ed Where's your red line gone? See? It's disappearing, isn't it?

Where's your Swiss Army knife. Have you lost it?

Christopher It's in my pocket.

Ed Where?

Christopher Here.

Ed How the hell are you going to find the Jubilee Line? You don't even know what an escalator is, do you?

Christopher It's a moving staircase. You step on to it. It carries you down. It's funny. Look.

Ed Stop laughing. Everybody's looking at you.

Christopher It's like something out of science fiction.

Ed I'm worried about you.

Christopher You're lying. You killed Wellington.

Ed Where are you going?

Christopher To watch the people. It's easy, look. You go to the black machine. You look at where you want to go. You find the price. You put your money in.

Ed You haven't got any money.

Christopher I have. I stole your card.

Ed You little shit.

Christopher You press Ticket Type. You press Adult Single. £2.20. You Insert £2.20. You Take Ticket and Change. You go up to the grey gate. You put your ticket in the slot. It comes out of the other side.

Customer Get a move on.

Ed There's no Jubilee Line. How are you going to get on the Jubilee Line to Willesden Green? You're in the wrong place.

Christopher There's a Bakerloo Line. Look. I can go to Willesden Junction.

Ed Come back home.

Christopher I can't.

Ed You can.

Christopher You told a lie. You killed Wellington. Swindon's not my home any more. My home is 451c Chapter Road, London NW2 5NG.

Ed *looks at him for a while.*

Ed Go to the left.

Christopher I know.

Ed The train will be very noisy.

Christopher I know.

Ed It'll really scare you.

Christopher I know.

Ed Try not to let it. Watch what the people do. Watch how they get on and off.

Christopher Yes.

The company stand with **Christopher** *on the platform.*

Ed Count the trains. Figure it out. Get the rhythm right.

Train coming. Train stopped. Train going. Silence. Train coming. Train stopped. Train going. Silence.

Christopher Train coming. Train stopped. Train going. Silence. Train coming. Train stopped. Train going. Silence.

Train coming. Train stopped. Train going. Silence.

Train coming. Train stopped. Train going. Silence.

Train coming. Train stopped. Train going. Silence.

Christopher *goes into his pocket. He can't find Toby.*

Christopher Toby?

He looks more. He can't find him. He panics. He stands up.

Toby? Where are you?

He explores the stage. He calls for Toby. He stays calm.

Toby? Toby? Toby. What are you doing down there?

He climbs down on to the tracks to rescue Toby.

Man with Socks Jesus. What are you doing?

Christopher My rat is on here.

Man with Socks Get out of there, for Christ's sake.

Christopher Toby . . . Toby . . . Toby . . .

Man with Socks Oh Christ. Oh Christ.

The **Man** *pulls* **Christopher** *off the tracks*. **Christopher** *screams for being touched. He calms. He puts Toby back in his pocket*.

Man with Socks What the hell do you think you were playing at?

Christopher I was finding Toby. He's my pet rat.

Man with Socks Bleeding Nora.[1]

Punk Girl Is he OK?

Man with Socks Him? Thanks a bundle. Jesus Christ. A pet rat. Oh shit. My train. Bollocks.

Punk Girl Are you OK?

She touches his arm. He screams.

OK. OK. OK. Is there anything I can do to help you?

1 Another colloquial expression of surprise or frustration.

Christopher Stand further away. I've got a Swiss Army knife and it has a saw blade and it could cut someone's finger off.

Punk Girl OK buddy. I'm going to take that as a no.

Punk Girl *and* **Man with Socks** *leave.* **Christopher** *counts the trains again.*

Christopher Train coming. Train stopped. Train going. Silence.

Train coming. Train stopped. Train going. Silence.

Train coming. Train stopped. Train going. Silence.

Is this train going to Willesden Junction?

Voice One There are 53,963 holiday cottages in Scandanavia and Germany.

Voice Two VITABIOTICS.

Christopher Is this train going to Willesden Junction?

Voice Three 3435.

Voice Five Penalty £10 if you fail to show a valid ticket for your entire journey.

Voice Four Discover Gold, Then Bronze.

Christopher Is this train going to Willesden Junction?

Voice One TVIC.

Voice Three EPBIC.

Voice Five Obstructing the doors can be dangerous.

Voice Two BRV.

Voice Three Con. IC.

Christopher Is this train going to Willesden Junction?

Voice Four TALK TO THE WORLD.

Voice One Warwick Avenue.

Maida Vale.

Kilburn Park.

Queen's Park.

Kensal Green.

Willesden Junction.[1]

Christopher Where is 451c Chapter Road, London NW2 5NG?

A **Shopkeeper** *shows him an A—Z of London.*

Shopkeeper A—Z of London. Two ninety-five.[2] Are you going to buy it or not?

Christopher I don't know.

Shopkeeper Well you can get your dirty fingers off it if you don't mind.

Christopher Where is 451c Chapter Road, London NW2 5NG?

Shopkeeper You can either buy the *A—Z* or you can hop it. I'm not a walking encyclopaedia.

Christopher Is that the *A—Z*?

Shopkeeper No, it's a sodding crocodile.

Christopher Is that the *A—Z*?

Shopkeeper Yes, it's the *A—Z*?

Christopher Can I buy it?

Shopkeeper Two pounds ninety-five, but you're giving me the money first. I'm not having you scarpering.

Christopher *examines the* A—Z. *He opens it. He looks for Chapter Road.*

A **Man on a Phone** *approaches him.*

1 Another cacophony of visual noise is occurring, although now Christopher is in the enclosed space of a tube train.

2 The A–Z is a printed street-map.

Man on Phone Big cheese. Oh yes. The nurses. Never. Bloody liar. Total. Bloody liar.

The **Man** *leaves.*

Christopher *closes the map. He stands up. He looks to the audience. He talks. His voice quietens the more he talks. And as he talks he squats. And then sits. And then huddles into a ball.*

Christopher Left. Right. Left. Right. Left. Right.

Left.

Right.

Left.

Right.

Left.

Right.

Left.

Christopher *sits silently, huddled for a while.*

Judy *and* **Roger** *enter.*

Judy I don't care whether you thought it was funny or not.

Roger Judy look, I'm sorry, OK.

Judy Well perhaps you should have thought about that before you made me look like a complete idiot.

Christopher *stands up.* **Judy** *sees him.*

The two look at one another.

Christopher You weren't in so I waited for you.

Judy Christopher.

Christopher What?

Judy Christopher.

She goes to hug him. He pushes her away so hard that he falls over.

Roger What the hell is going on?

Judy I'm so sorry, Christopher. I forgot.

Judy *spreads her fingers.* **Christopher** *spreads his to touch hands with her.*

Roger I suppose this means Ed's here.

Christopher *shows Toby to* **Roger**. **Roger** *recoils.*

Christopher He's hungry. Have you got any food I can give him and some water.

Judy Where's your father, Christopher?

Christopher I think he's in Swindon.

Roger Thank God for that.

Judy But how did you get here?

Christopher I came on the train.

Judy Oh my God, Christopher. I didn't . . . I didn't think I'd ever . . . Why are you here on your own?

Christopher, you're soaking. Roger, don't just stand there.

Roger Are you going to come in or are you going to stay out here all night?

Christopher I'm going to live with you because Father killed Wellington with a garden fork and I'm frightened of him.

Roger Jumping Jack Christ.[1]

Judy Roger, please. Come on. Christopher, let's go inside and get you dried off.

Go on or you'll catch your death.

Christopher *doesn't move.*

1 Another colloquial expression (slightly more forceful) of surprise or frustration.

Judy You follow Roger.

Christopher *doesn't move.*

Are you OK, Christopher?

Christopher I'm very tired.

Judy I know, love. Will you let me help you get your clothes off? I can get you a clean T-shirt. And some runners.[1]

You could get yourself into bed.

She changes him.

He wears one of her old T-shirts.

You're very brave.

Christopher Yes.

Judy You never wrote to me.

Christopher I know.

Judy Why didn't you write to me, Christopher? I wrote you all those letters. I kept thinking something dreadful had happened or you'd moved away and I'd never find out where you were.

Christopher Father said you were dead.

Judy What?

Christopher He said you went into hospital because you had something wrong with your heart. And then you had a heart attack and died.

Judy Oh my God.

Judy *starts to howl.*

Christopher Why are you doing that?

Judy Oh Christopher, I'm so sorry.

Christopher It's not your fault.

1 Jogging bottoms.

Judy Bastard. The Bastard.

Christopher, let me hold your hand. Just for once. Just for me. Will you? I won't hold it hard.

Christopher I don't like people holding my hand.

Judy No. OK. That's OK.

London Policeman I need to speak to him.

Judy He's been through enough today already.

London Policeman I know. But I still need to speak to him.

Christopher Boone. Please can you open the door.

Roger Come on, Christopher.

Judy Christopher love. It's all right. Just open the door, will you, sweetheart?

Christopher Is he going to take me away?

Judy No, Christopher, he isn't.

Christopher Will you let him take me away?

Judy No. I won't.

Christopher Do you promise?

Judy Yes. I promise.

London Policeman Your father says you've run away. Is that right?

Christopher Yes.

London Policeman Is this your mother?

Christopher Yes.

London Policeman Why did you run away?

Christopher Because Father killed Wellington who is a dog and so that meant that he could kill me.

London Policeman So I've been told. Do you want to go back to Swindon to your father or do you want to stay here?

Christopher I want to stay here.

London Policeman And how do you feel about that?

Christopher I want to stay here.

London Policeman Hang on, I'm asking your mother.

Judy He told Christopher I was dead.

London Policeman OK. Let's . . . let's not get into an argument about who said what here. I just want to know whether . . .

Judy Of course he can stay.

London Policeman Well, I think that probably settles it as far as I'm concerned.

Christopher Are you going to take me back to Swindon?

London Policeman No.

If your husband turns up and causes any trouble, just give us a ring. Otherwise you're going to have to sort this out amongst yourselves.

Ed I'm talking to her whether you like it or not.

Judy Roger. Don't. Just . . .

Roger I'm not going to be spoken to like that in my own home.

Ed I'll talk to you how I damn well like.

Judy You have no right to be here.

Ed He's my son in case you've forgotten.

Judy What in God's name did you think you were playing at saying those things to him?

Ed You were the one that bloody left.

Judy So, you decided to just wipe me out of his life altogether?

Roger Now let's just all calm down here, shall we?

Ed Well, isn't that what you wanted?

Judy I wrote to him every week.

Ed What is the bloody use is writing to him?

Roger Whoa. Whoa. Whoa.

Ed I cooked his meals. I cleaned his clothes. I looked after him every weekend. I looked after him when he was ill. I took him to the doctor. I worried myself sick every time he wandered off somewhere at night. I went to school every time he got into a fight. And you? What? You wrote him some sodding letters.

Christopher *gets up out of the sleeping bag.*

Judy So you thought it was OK to tell him his mother was dead?

Roger Now is not the time.

Christopher *finds his Swiss Army knife.*

Ed I'm going to see him. And if you try to stop me . . .

Ed *gets into* **Christopher***'s room.* **Christopher** *points his knife at him.*

Judy *comes in.*

Judy It's OK, Christopher, I won't let him do anything. You're all right.

Ed Christopher?

Ed *squats down, completely exhausted.*

Christopher *still points the knife at him.*

Ed Christopher I'm really, really sorry. About – About – About the letters. I never meant . . . I promise I will never do anything like that again.

Ed *spreads his fingers and tries to get* **Christopher** *to touch him.* **Christopher** *ignores him. He still holds his knife out. He groans.*

Ed Shit. Christopher, please.

London Policeman Mr Boone.

Ed What are you doing here? Did you call him?

London Policeman Mr Boone, come on mate.

Ed Don't bleeding mate me. This is my son.

London Policeman I know. This can all be sorted out. Just come with me. Please.

Judy I think you should go now. I think he's frightened.

Ed I'll be back.

Christopher. I'll be back. I promise you, Christopher. I promise you, lad.

Christopher *groans.*

London Policeman *watches* **Ed** *leave.*

Roger *watches them both leave.*

Judy *and* **Christopher** *are left alone together.*

Judy You go back to sleep now. Everything is going to be all right. I promise.

They leave **Christopher** *in his room. He lies down. He settles.*

Immediately he has settled it is the next morning. **Roger** *and* **Judy** *give* **Christopher** *breakfast. He is overwhelmed by them.*

Roger OK. He can stay for a few days.

Voice Three A plate of tomatoes.

Roger *gives him a plate of tomatoes.*

Judy He can stay as long as he needs to stay.

Voice Six Some egg whites.

Judy *gives him some egg whites.*

Roger This flat is hardly big enough for two people, let alone three.

Voice Four A tin of beans.

Roger *gives him a tin of beans.*

Judy He can understand what you're saying, you know?

Voice Five Tomato ketchup.

Judy *gives him tomato ketchup.*

Roger What's he going to do? There's no school for him to go to. We've both got jobs. It's bloody ridiculous.

Voice One A strawberry milkshake.

Roger *gives him a strawberry milkshake.*

Judy Roger. That's enough. You can stay as long as you want to stay.

Christopher It was Mother who gave me the milkshake.

They look at him.

It was Mother who gave me the milkshake, not you.

Judy *picks the milkshake up.*

Christopher You need to shout more loudly at him. Like you're really angry with him not just being nice.

Judy *looks at him. Nods.*

Judy OK.

She puts the milkshake down. She's much angrier.

Roger. That's enough. You can stay as long as you want to stay.

She looks at **Christopher***, examining his response. Expecting more feedback.*

Christopher I have to go back to Swindon.

They both look at him.

Judy Christopher, you've only just got here.

Christopher I have to go back because I have to sit my Maths A-Level.

Judy You're doing Maths A-Level?

Christopher Yes. I'm taking it on Wednesday and Thursday and Friday next week.

Judy God.

Christopher The Reverend Peters is going to be the invigilator.

Judy I mean that's really good.

Christopher I'm going to get an A grade. And that's why I have to go back to Swindon. Except I can't see Father. So I have to go back to Swindon with you.

Judy I don't know whether that's going to be possible.

Christopher But I have to go.

Judy Let's talk about this some other time, OK?

Christopher OK. But I have to go to Swindon.

He stands and leaves.

Judy Christopher. Please.

Christopher What time is it?

Siobhan Seven minutes past two in the morning.

Christopher I can't sleep.

Siobhan It's because you're scared of Mr Shears. You're being silly.

Christopher There's nobody about. You can hear traffic.

Christopher *wanders down the street.*

Siobhan What cars are there?

Christopher A Fiesta. A Nissan Micra. A Peugeot. A Ford Granada.

Siobhan What colours are they?

Christopher I can't tell. I can only see orange and black. And mixtures of orange and black.

Siobhan Look at the things people have in their front garden.

Christopher Oh yes. Is that an elf?

Siobhan It's a gnome. And a teddy bear. And a little pond, look.

Christopher And a cooker.

I like looking up at the sky.

Siobhan Me too.

Christopher When you look at the sky at night you know you are looking at stars, which are hundreds and thousands of light years away from you. And some of the stars don't exist any more because their light has taken so long to get to us that they are already dead, or they have exploded and collapsed into red dwarfs.[1] And that makes you seem very small, and if you have difficult things in your life it is nice to think that they are what is called negligible which means they are so small you don't have to take them into account when you are calculating something.

I can't see any stars here.

Siobhan No.

Christopher It's because of all the light pollution in London. All the light from the streetlights and car headlights and floodlights and lights in the buildings reflect off tiny particles in the atmosphere and they get in the way of light from the stars.

Two of the company approach. They talk in Ukrainian.

Ukrainian One *Ty wedel tovo malchika za mashynoy*? (Can you see that boy hiding behind the car?)

1 Red dwarfs are small, cool stars. They are the most common type of star in the Milky Way but, because of their size, they do not shine as brightly as other stars, meaning that it is not possible to see a red dwarf with the naked eye from Earth.

Christopher Who are they?

Siobhan Just strangers. Hide down between the skip and the van.

Ukrainian Two *Da, etot gorod polon grjobanykh sumashedshykh.* (Yes, I swear this city is full of crazy people.)

He hides.

They pass him, chatting in Ukrainian.

Christopher What language is that?

Siobhan I think it's Russian. Sshhh.

Christopher Have they gone? Have they gone? Have they gone? Did they see me?

Judy *starts looking for* **Christopher**.

Judy Christopher? Christopher?

Christopher *stands up*. **Judy** *stares at him.*

Judy Jesus Christ. What are you doing out here? I've been looking for you. I thought you'd gone. If you ever do that again, I swear to God, Christopher, I love you, but . . . I don't know what I'll do.

You need to promise me you won't leave the flat on your own again, Christopher. Christopher, do you promise me that?

Christopher Yes.

Judy You can't trust people in London.

Christopher Is it because they're strangers?

Roger Don't be a bloody fool.

Judy I'm not being a bloody fool, Roger, they got somebody in. They didn't even call me. They didn't ask me if I wanted to come back. I've been off two days. It's illegal that is.

Roger It was a temporary job, for Christ's sake.

Christopher I have to go to Swindon to take my A-Level.

Judy Christopher, not now.

I'm getting phone calls from your father threatening to take me to court. I'm getting it in the neck from Roger. It's not a good time.

Christopher But I have to go because it's been arranged and the Reverend Peters is going to invigilate.

Judy It's only an exam. I can ring the school. We can get it postponed. You can take it some other time.

Christopher I can't take it another time. It's been arranged. And I've done lots of revision. And Mrs Gascoyne says we could use a room at school.

Judy Christopher, I am just about holding this together. But I am this close to losing it, all right? So just give me some . . .

She breaks. She cries. She holds her fist to her mouth to try to stop herself.

She leaves the room. She comes back.

Judy Would you like an iced lolly?

Christopher Yes I would, please.

Judy Would you like a strawberry one?

Christopher Yes I would, please, because that's red. What's it called here?

Judy It's called Hampstead Heath. I love it. You can see all over London.

Christopher Where are the planes going to?

Judy Heathrow, I think.

Christopher, I rang Mrs Gascoyne.

I told her that you're going to take your Maths A-Level next year.

Christopher *screams. He throws his iced lolly away.*

Christopher, please. Calm down. OK. OK, Christopher. Just calm down, love.

Woman on Heath Is he OK?

Judy Well, what does it look like to you?

Christopher *screams and screams. He only stops because his chest hurts and he runs out of breath.*

Roger *gives* **Christopher** *a radio and three children's books.*

Roger Here we are. *100 Number Puzzles.* It's from the library. This one is called *The Origins of the Universe.* And this one is *Nuclear Power.*

Christopher They're for children.

They're not very good.

I'm not going to read them.

Roger Well, it's nice to know my contribution is appreciated.

Judy Christopher, I made you a chart. Because you've got to eat, love. In here is some Complan and it's got strawberry flavouring in it.[1]

Roger Complan?

Judy Be quiet, Roger. Christopher, if you drink 200 millilitres then I'm going to put a bronze star on your chart.

Roger I don't believe this.

Judy Roger, for God's sake, please. If you drink 400 millilitres you get a silver star.

Roger Ha!

1 Complan is a dietary supplement, typically given to elderly people to ensure that their diet includes the necessary nutrients.

Judy And if you drink 600 millilitres you get a gold star.

Roger A gold star. Well, that's very original I have to say.

Judy Roger, stop it.

Christopher *picks up the radio. He leaves. He de-tunes it so that it is between two stations. He listens to the white noise. He turns the volume up very high.*

Some time.

Roger *watches him. He opens and drinks four cans of lager. He necks the lager in one go.*

Roger *comes into his room. He is very drunk.*

Roger You think you're so bloody clever, don't you? Don't you ever, ever think about other people for one second, eh? Well, I bet you're really pleased with yourself now, aren't you?

He grabs at **Christopher**. **Christopher** *rolls himself into a ball to hide.*

Judy *comes into the room. She grabs* **Roger**. *She pulls him away from* **Christopher**.

Christopher *is moaning still in his ball.*

Judy Christopher, I'm sorry. I'm really, really sorry.

He remains in his ball.

He doesn't stop moaning.

Judy *and* **Roger** *leave.*

Eventually he calms.

Christopher What time is it?

Judy It's four o'clock.

Christopher What are you doing?

Judy I'm packing some clothes.

Christopher Where's Mr Shears?

Judy He's asleep.

Come downstairs. Bring Toby. Get into the car.

Christopher Into Mr Shears car?

Judy That's right.

Christopher Are you stealing the car?

Judy I'm just borrowing it.

Christopher Where are we going?

Judy We're going home.

Christopher Do you mean home in Swindon?

Judy Yes.

Christopher Is Father going to be there?

Judy Please, Christopher. Don't give me any hassle right now, OK?

Christopher I don't want to be with Father.

Judy Just . . . just . . . it's going to be all right, Christopher, OK? It's going to be all right.

Christopher Are we going back to Swindon so I can do my Maths A-Level?

Judy What?

Christopher I'm meant to be doing my Maths A-Level tomorrow.

Judy We're going back to Swindon because if we stay in London any longer . . . someone was going to get hurt. And I don't necessarily mean you.

Now I need you to be quiet for a while.

Christopher How long do you need me to be quiet for?

Judy Jesus. Half an hour, Christopher. I need you to be quiet for half an hour.

Ed How did you get in here?

Judy This is my house too, in case you've forgotten.

Ed Is your fancy man here, as well?

Christopher *gets a set of bongo drums out of one of the boxes. He begins drumming on them. He drums and drums and drums.*

Judy Christopher.

Christopher.

He's gone. You don't need to panic.

Christopher Where's he gone to?

Judy He's gone to stay with Rhodri for a while.

Christopher Is he going to be arrested? And go to prison?

Judy What for?

Christopher For killing Wellington.

Judy I don't think so. I think he'll only get arrested if Mrs Shears presses charges.

Christopher What's that?

Judy It's when you tell the police to arrest somebody for little crimes. They only arrest people for little crimes if you ask them.

Christopher Is killing Wellington a little crime?

Judy Yes love it is.

In the next few weeks we're going to try and get a place of our own to live in.

Christopher Can I do my Maths A-Level?

Judy You're not listening to me are you, Christopher?

Christopher I am listening to you.

Judy I told you. I rang your headmistress. I told her you were in London. I told her you'd do it next year.

Christopher But I'm here now so I can take it.

Judy I'm sorry, Christopher. I didn't know we'd be coming back. This isn't going to solve anything.

Mrs Shears You've got a bloody nerve.

Christopher Where are we going?

Mrs Shears Swanning round here as though nothing ever happened.

Judy Ignore her, Christopher.

Mrs Shears So has he finally dumped you too?

Christopher Where are we going?

Mrs Shears You had it coming. Don't try and pretend that you didn't. Because you bloody did.

Christopher Where are we going?

Judy We're going to the school.

Christopher *stops drumming.*

Siobhan So you're Christopher's mother.

Judy That's right. And you're . . .

Siobhan I'm Siobhan. It's nice to meet you.

Judy Yeah. Yes. Yes. It's nice to meet you too.

Siobhan Hello Christopher.

Christopher Hello.

Siobhan Are you OK?

Christopher I'm tired.

Judy He's a bit upset.

Siobhan Because of the A-Level, you said.

Judy He won't eat. He won't sleep.

Siobhan Yeah.

I spoke to Mrs Gascoyne after you called.

Judy Right.

Siobhan She still actually has your A-Level papers in the three sealed envelopes in her desk.

Mrs Gascoyne I still actually have the A-Level papers in my desk.

Christopher Does that mean I can still do my A-Level?

Siobhan I think so. We're going to ring the Reverend Peters to make sure he can still come in this afternoon. And Mrs Gascoyne is going to make a call to the examination board to say that you're going to take the exam after all. And hopefully they'll say that that's OK. But we can't know for sure. I thought I should tell you now. So you could think about it.

Christopher So I could think about what?

Siobhan Is this what you want to do, Christopher? If you say you don't want to do it no one is going to be angry with you. And it won't be wrong or illegal or stupid. It will just be what you want and that will be fine.

Christopher I want to do it.

Siobhan OK.

How tired are you?

Christopher Very.

Siobhan How's your brain when you think about maths?

Christopher I don't think it really works very well.

Siobhan What's the logarithmic formula for the approximate number of prime numbers not greater than x?[1]

Christopher I can't think.

Reverend Peters *enters. He picks up one envelope. He opens it. He looks at it. He carefully places it face down on* **Christopher***'s table.*

He goes to sit opposite him. He takes out a stopwatch.

Reverend Peters So young man, are we ready to roll?

Christopher *turns over the exam paper.*

He stares at it.

He can't understand any questions. He panics. His breathing becomes erratic. To calm himself he counts the cubes of cardinal numbers.[2]

Christopher 1, 8, 27, 64, 125, 216, 343, 512, 729, 1000, 1331.

Reverend Peters Are you all right, Christopher?

Christopher I can't read the question.

Reverend Peters What do you mean?

Christopher I can't read the question.

Reverend Peters Can you see the question?

Christopher I can see the questions but I can't read the questions because when I look at the words they all seem confused and the wrong way round and mixed up to me.

Reverend Peters Right.

Christopher What does this question say?

Reverend Peters Christopher, I'm afraid I can't help you like that. I'm not allowed to.

1 A logarithm is a mathematical tool designed to simplify complex calculations.

2 Cardinal numbers are numbers that say how much of something there is (e.g. 1, 2, 3, 4, 5 etc.). The cube of a number is itself multiplied three times: e.g. $2 \times 2 \times 2 = 8$, so the cube of 2 is 8.

Christopher *groans.*

Siobhan Christopher. Stop groaning. Get your breath. Count the cubes of the cardinal numbers again.

Christopher 1, 8, 27, 64, 125, 216, 343, 512, 729, 1000, 1331.

Siobhan Now. Have another go.

He looks at the questions again.

Christopher Show that a triangle with sides that can be written in the form $n^2 + 1$, $n^2 - 1$ and $2n$ (where n is greater than 1) is right-angled.

Siobhan You don't have to tell us.

Christopher What?

Siobhan You don't have to tell us how you solved it.

Christopher But it's my favourite question.

Siobhan Yes but it's not very interesting.

Christopher I think it is.

Siobhan Christopher, people won't want to hear about the answer to a maths question in a play.

Look, why don't you tell it after the curtain call?

When you've finished you can do a bow and then people who want to can go home and if anybody wants find out how you solved the maths question then they can stay and you can tell them at the end.

OK?

Christopher OK.

He picks up his pencil.

He starts answering.

Reverend Peters *Muchas Grazias, mio compadre.*[1] Make sure your name's on the front of the paper. Pop it in here. Don't panic.

1 'Many thanks, my friend'.

I'll have a quick word with the big man for you. And let's see what happens, shall we?

Ed *enters.*

Judy *is behind him.*

Ed Don't scream.

OK, Christopher. I'm not going to hurt you.

Ed *crouches down by* **Christopher**.

I wanted to ask you how the exam went.

Judy Tell him, Christopher.

Please, Christopher.

Christopher I don't know if I got all the questions right because I was really tired and I hadn't eaten any food so I couldn't think properly.

Ed *nods. There is some time.*

Ed Thank you.

Christopher What for?

Ed Just . . . thank you. I'm very proud of you, Christopher. Very proud. I'm sure you did really well.

Judy *gives* **Christopher** *the puzzle that she sent him.*

Christopher *successfully solves the puzzle, separating the two parts.*

Siobhan How's your flat?

Christopher It's not really a flat. It's a room. It's small. The corridor's painted brown. Other people use the toilet. Mother has to clean the toilet before I can use it. Sometimes there are other people in there so I do wet myself. The corridor smells like gravy and bleach. The room smells like socks and pine air freshener. I don't like waiting for my A-Level result.

If I was living at your house I would have room to put all my things and I wouldn't have to share the toilet with strangers.

Can I come and live in your house so that I'll have room to put all my things and I won't have to share the toilet with strangers?

Siobhan No, Christopher. You can't.

Christopher Why can't I? Is it because I'm too noisy and sometimes I'm 'difficult to control'.

Siobhan No. It's because I'm not your mother, Christopher.

Christopher No.

Siobhan That's very important, Christopher. Do you understand that?

Christopher I don't know.

Mother doesn't get back from work till 5.30. So I have to go to Father's house between 3.49 and 5.30 because I'm not allowed to be on my own. Mother said I didn't have a choice. I pushed the bed up against the door in case Father tries to come in. Sometimes he tries to talk to me through the door. I don't answer him. Sometimes he sits outside the door quietly for a long time.

Ed *enters. He's holding a kitchen timer.*

Ed Christopher, can I have a talk with you?

Christopher *turns away from* **Siobhan**.

Christopher No. No. No. No. No. No, you can't. No.

Judy It's OK. I'll be here.

Christopher I don't want to talk to Father.

Ed I'll do you a deal. Five minutes, OK? That's all. Then you can go.

Ed *sets the timer for five minutes. It starts ticking.*

Christopher, look . . . Things can't go on like this. I don't know about you, but this . . . this just hurts too much. You being in the house but refusing to talk to me. You have to learn to trust me . . . And I don't care how long it takes . . . if it's a minute one day and two minutes the next and three minutes the next and it takes years I don't care. Because this is important. This is more important than anything else. Let's call it . . . let's call it a project. A project we have to do together. You have to spend more time with me. And I . . . I have to show you that you can trust me. And it will be difficult at first because . . . because it's a difficult project. But it will get better, I promise. You don't have to say anything, not right now. You have to think about it. And . . . I've got you a present. To show you that I really mean what I say. And to say sorry. And because . . . well you'll see what I mean.

Ed *leaves.*

He comes back with a big cardboard box. It is importantly cardboard and different to the other boxes. There's a blanket in it. He puts his hands in the box. He takes out a little sandy-coloured Golden Retriever.

He's two months old.

The dog sits on **Christopher***'s lap.*

Judy You won't be able to take him away with you, I'm afraid. The bedsit's too small. But your father's going to look after him here. And you can come and take him out for walks whenever you want.

Christopher Does he have a name?

Ed No. You can decide what to call him.

Christopher Sandy. He's called Sandy.

The alarm goes off.

They look at each other.

Judy We need to go now.

Ed Yes.

Judy We'll come back tomorrow and you can see him then.

Siobhan Christopher.

Christopher Yes.

Siobhan Here.

Christopher What's this?

Siobhan It's your result, Christopher.

Christopher Right.

Siobhan You need to open it and read it.

Christopher Right.

He does.

Siobhan Well? What does it say?

Christopher I got an A.

Siobhan Oh. Oh. That's just. That's terrific, Christopher.

Christopher Yes.

Siobhan Aren't you happy?

Christopher Yes. It's the best result.

Siobhan I know it is. How's your dog?

Christopher He's very well. I stayed last week at Father's because Mother got flu and he slept on my bed so he can bark in case anybody comes into my room at night.

Siobhan Right. How are you getting on with your father, Christopher?

Christopher He planted a vegetable patch in his garden. I helped him and Sandy watched. We planted carrots and peas and spinach and I'm going to pick them when they're ready. He bought me a book, which is called *Further Maths for A-Level*. He told Mrs Gascoyne that I'm going to take Further Maths next year. She said OK.

Mrs Gascoyne OK.

Siobhan I heard that.

Christopher I'm going to pass it and get an A grade. And then in two years I'll take A-Level Physics and get an A grade. And then I'm going to go to university in another town. It doesn't have to be in London because I don't like London and there are universities in lots of places and not all of them are in big cities. I can live in a flat with a garden and a proper toilet. I can take Sandy and my books and my computer. Then I will get a First-Class Honours degree. Then I will be a scientist. I can do these things.

Siobhan I hope so.

Christopher I can because I went to London on my own.

She looks at him.

I solved the mystery of Who Killed Wellington.

She looks at him.

I found my mother. I was brave.

Siobhan You were.

Christopher And I wrote a book.

Siobhan I know. I read it. We turned it into a play.

Christopher Yes. Does that mean I can do anything, do you think?

Does that mean I can do anything, Siobhan?

Does that mean I can do anything?

The two look at each other for a while.

Lights black.

After the curtain call **Christopher** *returns to the stage. He gets the attention of anybody still in the audience.*

Postscript

Christopher Thank you very much for clapping and thank you very much for staying behind to listen to how I answered the question on my Maths A-level. Siobhan said it wouldn't be very interesting but I said it was.

She didn't tell me what I should use, so I decided to use everything in the theatre including VL000 arc lights, which are moving lights, a smoke machine, light-emitting diodes, UBL control speakers, an overhead projector and a woman called a deputy stage manager who will operate these.

The lights referred to should be the actual lights used in the production and these references should change accordingly.

I had ninety minutes to answer ten questions – but I spent thirty minutes doing groaning which meant I only had six minutes to answer this question.

A timer may be projected, displaying 6.00.00.

And this is what I wrote.

Christopher *starts the timer. A right-angled triangle, made using lasers, might float above* **Christopher** *and slowly lower around him. If this is not possible the triangle could be made by projection or by the company.*

'Prove the following:

'A triangle with sides that can be written in the form $n^2 + 1$, $n^2 - 1$ and $2n$ (where n is bigger than 1) is right-angled.'

If the triangle is right-angled, one of its angles will be 90 degrees and will therefore follow Pythagoras's theorem.[1]

According to Pythagoras:
(*Company sing/rap/* **Christopher** *with delay.)*
If the sum of the squares of the two shorter sides
Equals the square of the hypotenuse
Then the triangle is
Then the triangle is
Then the triangle is
Right-angled.

Pythagoras said that $a^2 + b^2 = c^2$.

To put it simply, if you draw squares outside the three sides of a right-angled triangle, then add up the area of the two smaller squares, this will be equal to the area of the larger square. This is only true if the triangle is a right-angled triangle.

A projected diagram may show this at this point.

The A-level question is an algebraic formula for making right-angled triangles. Algebra is like a computer programme that works for whatever numbers you put into it.

I have to show that a triangle with sides whose lengths are $n^2 + 1$, $n^2 - 1$ and $2n$ (where n is bigger than 1) is right-angled.

To find the area of the squares you have to multiply one of the sides by itself. I must show that the area of the squares on the two shorter sides adds up to the square on the long side.

This means doing some algebra.

1 Pythagoras was a Greek philosopher and mathematician who lived during the fifth and sixth centuries BC.

A formula representing the necessary mathematical equation may appear at this point.

Let me show you.

He refers to the demonstrated triangle.

To find the area of $2n$, we simply multiply $2n$ by $2n$. This equals $4n^2$.

He refers to the triangle again.

As he solves the problem so any demonstration of triangle or equation might change to follow the solution.

To find the area of $n^2 - 1$, we must multiply $n^2 - 1$ by $n^2 - 1$.

I will draw lines on the equation to show what is multiplied.

(Stupid people at my school get very confused at this point. Although I am not allowed to call them stupid even though that is what they are.)

That gives me n to the power of four $- 2n^2 + 1$.

Now I must add these together:

n to the power of $4 + 4n^2 - 2n^2 + 1 = n$ to the power of $4 + 2n^2 + 1$.

If the triangle is right-angled, this answer should be equal to the area of the larger square. Let's check:

$n^2 + 1 \times n^2 + 1 = n$ to power of $4 + 2n^2 + 1$.

So the areas of the two small squares add up to the area of the large square. So all my squares fit together to satisfy Pythagoras's theorem. So the triangle is right-angled.

Now let's check this proof with some examples:

If $n = 2$, the triangle has lengths 3, 4 and 5, and $3^2 + 4^2$ is $9 + 16$ which is 25 which is 5^2.

If $n = 3$, the sides of the triangle are 8, 6 and 10, and $8^2 + 6^2$ is $64 + 36$ which is 100 which is 10^2.

$n = 4$: the sides of the triangle are 15, 8 and 17, and $15^2 + 8^2$ is $225 + 64$ which is 289 which is 17^2.

$n = 5$: the sides of the triangle are 24, 10 and 26, and $24^2 + 10^2$ is $576 + 100$ which is 676 which is 26^2.

$n = 6$: the sides of the triangle are 35, 12 and 37, and $35^2 + 12^2$ is $1225 + 144$ which is 1369 which is 37^2.

My proof shows why this works for every n.

Quod erat demonstrandum.

And that is how I got an A grade!!!